How to Show & Sell Your Crafts

How To Show & Sell Your Crafts

The crafter's complete guide on how to display work at shows and make *profitable* sales

Kathryn Caputo

BETTERWAY BOOKS
CINCINNATI, OHIO

Acknowledgments

My special thanks to David Lewis, Greg Albert, Julie Wesling Whaley, Marilyn Daiker and the entire F&W Publications staff for their constant support, patience and guidance.

Dedicated to the many ambassadors of the crafts industry—crafters, show producers, manufacturers, retailers and publishers working in harmony for the betterment of that industry.

01   00   99   98   97   5   4   3   2   1

Library of Congress Cataloging-in-Publication Data

Caputo, Kathryn.
    How to show & sell your crafts / by Kathryn Caputo.
        p.   cm.
    Includes index.
    ISBN 1-55870-447-7 (pbk.: alk. paper)
    1. Decorative arts—United States—Marketing. 2. Handicraft—United States—Marketing. I. Title.
NK805.C36   1997
745.5′068′8—dc21   97-23813
                                                                                          CIP

Editor: Julie Wesling Whaley
Production editor: Marilyn Daiker
Interior designer: Brian Roeth
Cover designer: Stephanie Redman

About the Author

Kathryn Caputo lives in Bethel, Connecticut, with her fifteen-year-old daughter, Chrissy. She has been an active crafter for more than ten years but didn't take crafting seriously until 1989 when she lost her full-time job.

Disenchanted with the corporate life, and not wanting to once again start at "the bottom of the ladder" or put her future into someone else's hands, Kathy turned to crafting as a full-time business. Finally, she could set her own business hours, be more available to meet her daughter's needs, and satisfy her won creative spirit—all from the comforts of her own home.

Participating in craft shows ultimately led to producing craft shows of her own. To date, Kathy has produced and promoted more than forty craft shows in her own and neighboring states. She has also produced shows for other industries. Kathy is the author of *How to Start Making Money With Your Crafts*.

Table of Contents

Introduction

Many new crafters venture into the crafts marketplace with such wonderfully innovative products and such beautiful designs that you would think their sales success would be guaranteed. Yet they may experience only limited and even disappointing sales. Often, these new crafters become frustrated and abandon their crafts business for other, more traditional ways to make money.

But there is a reason why some crafters succeed where others fail. And it may have less to do with the actual crafts product itself than you would think. Often, it is simply a matter of *marketing*. Creating an effective marketing campaign will help you show and sell your products to their best advantage.

How to Show & Sell Your Crafts provides examples of tried-and-true marketing techniques that will help take your fledgling crafts business to new heights of success. This book is as much about image-building as it is about building your crafts business. The two go hand in hand. It is not only what you make that is important, but also how you, your products and your crafts company are *perceived* that can make the difference between mediocre sales and great sales.

In Part One, "How to Market Your Products, Your Business and Yourself," you will learn how to conduct effective market research; ways to add market *value* to your products; techniques to better publicize your crafts business and even how to build a stronger public image of yourself as a crafter.

Part Two, "How to Display Your Crafts," focuses on craft shows, but also includes commercial selling environments. With craft and product-specific examples of individual display components and suggestions for setup designs and arrangements, you will be able to make the most of your allotted display area. Your products will be more readily visible to your customers and that cannot help but result in better sales.

Part Three, "Salesmanship," will fine-tune your selling skills by showing you ways to *connect* with your customers at crafts shows—what to do and what to say—to develop a rapport and encourage interest in you and your products.

If you employ all or even most of the displaying and selling techniques outlined in this book, you should find that your sales will increase. You will move from the ranks of "beginner crafter" with just mediocre sales toward the status of "professional crafter" with increased and more consistent returns and a better understanding of your market.

SALE!

**DEVELOP
SALESMANSHIP SKILLS**
- Know what to *do*
- Know what to *say*

**ACCENT YOUR DISPLAY
WITH "SOFTWARE"**
- Color
- Visual aids
- Audio accents
- Dress for success

**DESIGN AN EFFECTIVE CRAFTS
SHOW DISPLAY**
- *Showcase* your products and craft
- Make it customer and crafter friendly
- Give it height, composition and balance
- Make it flexible, portable, sturdy and stable
- Stock it with sufficient inventory
- Give it personality and ambiance

MARKET YOURSELF
- Develop a good *reputation*
- Use the media to *publicize* yourself and your business
- Take every opportunity to gain public *exposure*

MARKET YOUR BUSINESS
- Build a successful image for your business
- Use sales tools to promote and advertise your business

FIND YOUR NICHE
- In your price range
- In your product market
- In your craft market

PRICE AND VALUE YOUR PRODUCTS COMPETITIVELY AND CORRECTLY
- Cover your expenses
- Build in a reasonable profit margin
- Adjust your price to reflect the current fair-market value

CREATE A FINE PRODUCT
- Neat, complete and unique
- Store quality
- *Handmade* not homemade

RESEARCH YOUR MARKET
- Know your *product* market
- Know your *craft* market
- Know your *customers*

Part One

HOW TO MARKET YOUR

PRODUCT, YOUR BUSINESS

AND YOURSELF

What Is Marketing?

What is *marketing?* Often, marketing and *selling* are used synonymously to mean the exchange of money for product between buyer and seller. But marketing is so much more than the selling transaction itself. It is the step that comes *before* the sale. It is putting together the right combination of product, presentation and pricing, and offering that package to the right customer base.

Marketing is what leads the customer to that final decision to buy. It is the *art* of selling. And the sale is the result of good marketing strategy and effective market research.

Crafters are, by nature, resourceful and imaginative. Their products are usually unique and interesting. So thinking up ways to effectively market your crafts should be almost as much fun as making them. Simply apply your creative abilities to the promotion of your finished product and not just to its construction and design.

But many crafters leave their imaginations at the door when it comes to marketing their very special creations. They assume their products will simply sell themselves. Maybe so, but would you like to stake your income on it or would you rather do everything in your power to make sure the customer gets interested enough in your products to buy?

And as important as the product itself is the *presentation* of that product to the public. How it is displayed, what you tell your customers about it, how your advertising and promotional literature is designed and how it reads, and even how you present yourself—can all add market *value* to your products and sales dollars to your pocketbook.

If both the product and the presentation are on target, but the price is set either too high to be competitive or too low for the buyer to respect the value of your product, then the results will be the same. No (or very few) sales. Without correct pricing, the best products in the world, with the best packaging and presentation in the world, may not ever be sold. Creative pricing is just another way to add market value to your products.

There is a great deal of competition in the crafts world. The industry is growing in leaps and bounds. New crafters are being ''born'' every day. So it is important that you not only craft a fine product but also that you craft a credible *image* of yourself and your crafts business to further the market potential of the products you sell. And you should market that image as aggressively as you do your products.

Many not-so-wonderful products have been sold successfully by employing effective marketing techniques and offering the customer just the right package of product, presentation and pricing. And many truly innovative products have gathered dust on the shelves for lack of it.

The next, and no less important, consideration in marketing your products successfully is to know your customer. You should have a very clear image of *who* will be buying your products. How can you make the right product choices, present them effectively and price them correctly if you have no idea who your customers are, what they like, what they need, what they can afford or where to find them? Once you have a clear picture of your customer, you can tailor your marketing campaign to appeal to the audience you are trying to attract.

And, as if that weren't enough, you must keep constant vigil over both the crafts and consumer marketplace to make sure that times and trends don't shift without your being aware of it, causing your products to lose some of their market value.

Now this may all sound very tedious and you might say to yourself, ''Gosh, I'm only a *crafter*! What do I know about *marketing*?'' But really, creating a marketing campaign and conducting market research can be fascinating. And knowing it could substantially increase your sales should motivate you to take some time to explore the possibilities. You'll be amazed at what you will learn and how the information you gather will affect your selling strategy and the future success of your crafts business.

Successful marketing is putting together the right package of product, presentation and pricing *and offering that package to the right customer base.*

Market Research

When I started selling crafts about ten years ago, I just made products *I* liked and then went to crafts shows and tried to sell them. Actually, I tried for two seasons to sell my products with little or no success. Discouraged and disheartened, I almost gave up my crafts business altogether. It was costing me money I could not afford. Though I really enjoyed what I was doing, I was tired of making the effort and not reaping the rewards. Does that sound at all familiar?

But I made the decision to hold on for just one more season and to do some investigating before I quit. I wanted to know *why* I wasn't as successful as so many other crafters. If they could do it, why couldn't I?

First I started asking questions at every crafts show I participated in, of every customer who came my way. "What do you like? What do you need? How much would you be willing to pay for it?" I picked the brains of every veteran crafter to gain information. "How long have you been selling crafts? Did you always make the same products? What crafts shows do you participate in? What show did you do last week? How was it? What products sold best there? What kind of customers came? Did you see my type of product there? How did it sell?"

I observed crafters at other shows who sold similar products but were much more successful than me. How did they display their products? What did they say to their customers? How did they act? What did they wear? I watched the customers. How did they respond to the crafter? Did they buy?

I visited retail stores and studied commercial products similar to mine.

Were they larger? Smaller? More expensive? Less expensive? How were they designed and constructed? What colors were used? Did people buy them?

I read home decorating and women's magazines (or at least looked at the pictures) to determine which styles and decorative trends were popular so I could add their flavor to my own work. While I did all this, I took notes on what I saw, read and heard.

Though at the time I never would have termed what I was doing as "market research," that's exactly what it was. Market research is finding out as much as you can about everything having to do with your product, your craft, your industry, the market and your customers. And market research taught me a great deal about why my products weren't selling. It was really quite a revelation (and a humbling experience) to find out that there wasn't just one reason, but many reasons.

It appeared at first that I really hadn't been doing anything right! After reviewing all of my information, I was surprised I had sold any product at all. The only positive encouragement I received was in finding I had made a good product choice: Christmas tree skirts. So, the product was fine, but basically everything else had to go.

Through my market research, I learned exactly what needed to be changed and how to change it in order to make my products competitive and my crafts business successful. I needed to:

1. Change the size and color of my products.
2. Make more of them—in a greater variety of designs.
3. Create a new and more professional crafts show display.
4. Raise my prices.
5. Participate in better crafts shows.

One by one, I made these changes. And as I did, I saw an increase in my sales—and profit. As I implemented and fine-tuned my marketing plan, guided by my market research, the money I made increased proportionately.

As you conduct your market research, you too will probably be surprised at what you learn, though I hope not to as great an extent as I was. You will also find that if you *use* the insight gleaned from your market research, your sales will increase significantly.

First, recognize that none of us lives in a vacuum. We are all affected in one way or another by what goes on around us. Changes in the economy and in the workplace, shifts in sociological structures and many other factors, all affect *how* people buy merchandise, *what* they buy, *how much* they can afford to spend and even *where* and *when* they shop for the products they do buy. In other words, everything that affects your customers can ultimately affect your sales. There's a great big world out there—outside of the crafts industry. Learn about it, understand it and use what you learn to increase your sales.

You need to know which products are selling and which are not. Which crafts and product categories are saturated and which are not. What is the "going rate" (price) for a particular product? What crafts are consumers most interested in buying *now*? What craft products are being mass-produced at discount prices? And just because a craft or product is popular in one part of the country doesn't mean it is or ever will be popular in your part of the country. You need to know what is selling—when and where.

The object of your market research is to
- Know your crafts and their value
- Know your products and their value
- Know your customers and what they will pay for your crafts and your products

---

Tracking popular consumer trends, learning about the life-styles and current attitudes of your customers, researching the current crafts and general merchandise markets, and analyzing where your product fits into those markets, are all part of market research. They tell you the things that interest your customers *now*. You need to have this information to develop products that will suit these customers and meet the needs of a changing society.

Market research, more than any other single factor, will help you make a success of your crafts business. Presenting the right product, at the right time, at the right price, to the right consumer audience is no accident. It takes planning. Marketing is a strategy game.

Market research is also an ongoing endeavor. It is not something you do once and then forget about. Times change. People's needs change. Customers' tastes change. In order to be competitive in any marketplace you should be ever aware of these changes.

By now you are probably saying something like "Gee, this sounds a little too much like *work*!" Well, if you want to be successful in your crafts business, you need to really work at it. This doesn't mean you shouldn't enjoy your crafts, but wouldn't it be even more fun if you made more money from your efforts? Wouldn't you rather bring home $1,000 to $4,000 from a six-hour crafts show than just break even? Sure sounds like fun to me!

The Market

Let's ease into this thing called "market research" slowly by taking a broad look at the consumer marketplace and your commercial competition. Then we'll move a little closer to home and study the crafts marketplace and your more immediate competition—your fellow crafters. Researching both markets is essential to your sales success. Researching only one or the other will give you a distorted market image that can send your crafts business careening in the wrong direction.

The Consumer Marketplace and Commercial Competition

Ultimately, there is a mass-produced version of almost every product the crafts industry has to offer. Now, don't get offended, these products may not be exactly the same as yours, but in some cases they may be close enough in the consumer's eyes to warrant purchasing a mass-produced product over a crafter-made product.

Though you shouldn't consider yourself in direct competition with the commercial market and its store-sold and mass-produced products, understand that commercial trends can seriously impact craft sales. As crafters, we indirectly compete with the variety and diversity of commercial products, the lower-priced nature of these goods and the convenience of retail shopping.

PRODUCT COMPETITION

Once the commercial market picks up on a popular crafts product and starts to manufacture and mass-market it, the crafter who makes that type of product may have a more difficult time selling it. The market becomes saturated with many different versions and quality levels of the same product. The uneducated consumer often can't tell the difference in quality—only in price.

Now, I know you might be thinking, "We make crafts products designed for the discriminating buyer who is looking for something special!" Often, crafters take the easy road of assembling products that bear too strong a resemblance to their mass-produced counterparts rather than actually creating a product that *is* unique and different. Shoppers come to crafts shows to buy what they cannot buy anywhere else. If they can buy the same product somewhere else, they won't need to buy it from you. A sobering thought.

Always remember . . . Consumers come to crafts shows to buy what they cannot buy anywhere else. If they can find it somewhere else, they won't need to buy it from you.

SHOPPING CONVENIENCE

Consumers can purchase almost any product from one of the home shopping networks, from any one of a hundred conveniently located stores open six or seven days and evenings a week, via mail order or even on the Internet. From "handmade" quilts to pottery, it's out there somewhere in the commercial marketplace.

Craft customer exposure, on the other hand, is limited mostly to weekend crafts shows. Customers have to make a concerted effort to go to a crafts show. They have to plan their shopping and their time to coincide with the crafts events they wish to attend. This can be inconvenient.

Make it as easy as possible for customers to buy your products. Offer them alternatives such as mail order service and credit card acceptance.

Though you still need to sell at crafts shows, providing these services will make you more competitive in the overall marketplace.

PRICE

Most mass-produced products are also cheaper than crafts products, though they may not be as well made or quite as lovely. With most of America watching their pennies and looking for the best value for their dollar, price is often a deciding factor for the consumer.

While many consumers prefer to buy a handmade version of an already mass-produced product just because it is handmade, others see the higher-priced handmade product as superfluous. Why should they pay more for basically the same product just because it was made by a crafter? Not a good enough reason.

Price your products competitively and reasonably within the parameters of your market. This will afford you the best chance for success.

While mass-produced products in the commercial marketplace compete indirectly with you for consumer dollars, your more immediate competition comes from your fellow crafters. And they can really give you a run for your money.

The Crafts Marketplace and Peer Competition

The crafts marketplace, our own little corner of the consumer marketplace, is really not so small. There are tens of thousands of crafters out there doing what you are doing—making and selling crafts. The variety of products and craft techniques is astounding. Competition among crafters is keen. There are only a limited number of weekends in a year, a limited number of crafts shows in one area in one weekend, and only so many spaces available at each crafts show. How will you compete?

COMPETING FOR ADMISSION TO SHOWS

A crafts show producer sifts through hundreds of show applications and product photographs trying to select the best variety of products for admission to their shows.

Traditionally, jewelry crafts dominate the crafts market. Florals and wood crafts run a close second to jewelry, and fabric products are also popular. Now, these are all very general descriptions of just a few of the major crafts categories but, if you were a show producer, you must limit each craft category to 5 percent or at most 10 percent of your total number of crafters. If your show held space for sixty crafters, then only three to six of them could be jewelry vendors—or wood vendors—or floral crafters—in order to have a diversified and interesting show. If you were a show producer, how would you decide which applications to accept and which to decline? And how will you, as a crafter, cope with this competition? What would make a show producer choose your entry over another?

If you know your product or craft category to be a popular one, here are two ways to get a slight edge on your competition. (1) Apply early to the shows you want to attend. Sometimes, postmark can be the deciding factor. (2) Send clear, uncluttered, good-quality photographs or slides (whichever is requested) of your product and your show display with your application. If they are undecided about your products, an impressive display presentation might sway them in your favor.

AT THE SHOW

Just being accepted to a show doesn't guarantee sales at the show. It just gets your foot in the door. Most likely, other crafters will sell products that will somehow compete with yours, especially if it is a very large show.

The more you know about your competition—in advance of the show—the better your sales will be at the show. Go to other craft shows as a observer. Research competing products and prices. Research similar craft techniques. Study the crafts market in general. Fine-tune your crafting skills. Find out what's already being sold out there and how successfully it is selling. Find out what there is too much (or too little) of. Right now in today's market, certain craft/product categories are more competitive and saturated than others. Know which ones are and which are not. Know your competition.

Remember you and your fellow crafters are not only *competitors*, but also *allies*. You work within and promote the same industry. You have the same basic needs and goals. You work side by side, booth to booth, weekend after weekend. Make it a pleasant experience for all concerned. Don't let the weight of competition alter your perception of these people. They are trying to make a living—same as you.

Conducting Market Research

Conducting market research is easier than you would imagine—and quite interesting. But you can't go off with just a vague idea of what you are looking for and how to find it. You have to have a plan and an organized, systematic way of recording the information you gather. Later, you will draw logical conclusions from this data.

Prepare a list of questions to ask yourself as you go from store to store . . . from mail-order catalog to mail-order catalog . . . from crafts show to crafts show . . . to help organize your findings and make it easier to draw *correct* conclusions from your market research. When you have completed the first round of research, you should know where your current products stand in today's market and what you need to change to become more competitive and more successful.

In a nutshell, you will be gathering information about your product market, your craft market and your customers. You will also look to identify two things: *competition* from similar products and *gaps* in the market—voids where no or very few products fill an existing need.

 When conducting market research, identify two things:
1. *Competition* from similar products
2. *Gaps* where no or few products fill an existing need

Know Your Product Market

Select one principal product from your product line and ask yourself, ''How well do I know this product's market?'' Put a check mark next to your answer.

☐ Very well

☐ Not very well

☐ Fairly well

☐ Hardly at all

Then copy and take the simple quiz on pages 18-19. It's just a list of questions to confirm your product knowledge. If you don't know an answer, leave it blank. Do not speculate. You can't guess at important market information—you have to know it.

Select selling environments that are familiar to you. For example, for a "Department Store," write the name of a store you shop frequently. Don't go there, just answer the questions from what you remember. Fill in your answers under the heading "Before MR" (before Market Research).

After you have taken the quiz, visit or study the actual selling environments you selected. Then take the quiz again, this time entering your answers in the second column under the heading "After MR" (after Market Research). Give yourself two points for each correct answer—each answer where your "before" answer (what you thought) matches your "after" answer (what actually is). Total your score. Now go back and answer my original question: "How well did you know your product market?

☐ Very well (score 80-100)

☐ Fairly well (score 60-79)

☐ Not well (score 40-59)

☐ Hardly at all (below 40)

This is not, by any means the end of your product market research, but it is a good beginning. It will give you an idea of what important information you may have overlooked. For each product, there will be other questions relative only to that product. Start with the basics and add any and all questions that might help you make better and more educated product decisions.

Other things I need to know about my product market:

1. _____

2. _____

3. _____

Don't limit your market research to selling environments you know. The very basis of market research is to find out what you *don't* know. Use this quiz as a survey when exploring other unfamiliar selling environments. And do explore them. Use it for each and every product you sell.

Know Your Craft Market

Some crafts are "hot" and new; others have always been popular and in the mainstream (quilting, woodworking, florals, pottery and jewelry making); some seem to go in and out of center stage with great peaks and

PRODUCT	BEFORE MR *(market research)*	AFTER MR *(market research)*	SCORE

MAJOR DEPARTMENT STORE:

Does this store carry my product?	☐ Yes ☐ No	☐ Yes ☐ No
What is the price?	$_____	$_____
Does their product look like mine?	☐ a little ☐ just like ☐ not much	☐ a little ☐ just like ☐ not much
Size: Is theirs . . .	☐ larger ☐ smaller ☐ same size	☐ larger ☐ smaller ☐ same size
Construction/Quality/Design: Is theirs . . .	☐ better ☐ equal ☐ inferior	☐ better ☐ equal ☐ inferior

GENERAL MERCHANDISE STORE:

Does this store carry my product?	☐ Yes ☐ No	☐ Yes ☐ No
What is the price?	$_____	$_____
Does their product look like mine?	☐ a little ☐ just like ☐ not much	☐ a little ☐ just like ☐ not much
Size: Is theirs . . .	☐ larger ☐ smaller ☐ same size	☐ larger ☐ smaller ☐ same size
Construction/Quality/Design: Is theirs . . .	☐ better ☐ equal ☐ inferior	☐ better ☐ equal ☐ inferior

DISCOUNT STORE:

Does this store carry my product?	☐ Yes ☐ No	☐ Yes ☐ No
What is the price?	$_____	$_____
Does their product look like mine?	☐ a little ☐ just like ☐ not much	☐ a little ☐ just like ☐ not much
Size: Is theirs . . .	☐ larger ☐ smaller ☐ same size	☐ larger ☐ smaller ☐ same size
Construction/Quality/Design: Is theirs . . .	☐ better ☐ equal ☐ inferior	☐ better ☐ equal ☐ inferior

SPECIALTY STORE/GIFT SHOP:

Does this store carry my product?	☐ Yes ☐ No	☐ Yes ☐ No
What is the price?	$_____	$_____
Does their product look like mine?	☐ a little ☐ just like ☐ not much	☐ a little ☐ just like ☐ not much
Size: Is theirs . . .	☐ larger ☐ smaller ☐ same size	☐ larger ☐ smaller ☐ same size
Construction/Quality/Design: Is theirs . . .	☐ better ☐ equal ☐ inferior	☐ better ☐ equal ☐ inferior

MAIL-ORDER CATALOG:

Does this store carry my product?	☐ Yes ☐ No	☐ Yes ☐ No
What is the price?	$_____	$_____
Does their product look like mine?	☐ a little ☐ just like ☐ not much	☐ a little ☐ just like ☐ not much
Size: Is theirs . . .	☐ larger ☐ smaller ☐ same size	☐ larger ☐ smaller ☐ same size
Construction/Quality/Design: Is theirs . . .	☐ better ☐ equal ☐ inferior	☐ better ☐ equal ☐ inferior

PRODUCT	BEFORE MR *(market research)*	AFTER MR *(market research)*	SCORE
FLEA MARKET:			
Is my product sold at flea markets?	☐ Yes ☐ No	☐ Yes ☐ No	
What is the price?	$_____	$_____	
Does their product look like mine?	☐ a little ☐ just like ☐ not much	☐ a little ☐ just like ☐ not much	
Size: Is theirs . . .	☐ larger ☐ smaller ☐ same size	☐ larger ☐ smaller ☐ same size	
Construction/Quality/Design: Is theirs . . .	☐ better ☐ equal ☐ inferior	☐ better ☐ equal ☐ inferior	
HOME SHOPPING NETWORK:			
Do they sell my product?	☐ Yes ☐ No	☐ Yes ☐ No	
What is the price?	$_____	$_____	
Does their product look like mine?	☐ a little ☐ just like ☐ not much	☐ a little ☐ just like ☐ not much	
Size: Is theirs . . .	☐ larger ☐ smaller ☐ same size	☐ larger ☐ smaller ☐ same size	
Construction/Quality/Design: Is theirs . . .	☐ better ☐ equal ☐ inferior	☐ better ☐ equal ☐ inferior	
THE INTERNET:			
Is my product sold on the Internet?	☐ Yes ☐ No	☐ Yes ☐ No	
What is the price?	$_____	$_____	
Does their product look like mine?	☐ a little ☐ just like ☐ not much	☐ a little ☐ just like ☐ not much	
Size: Is theirs . . .	☐ larger ☐ smaller ☐ same size	☐ larger ☐ smaller ☐ same size	
Construction/Quality/Design: Is theirs . . .	☐ better ☐ equal ☐ inferior	☐ better ☐ equal ☐ inferior	
CRAFTS SHOW:			
Have I seen my product at crafts shows?	☐ Yes ☐ No	☐ Yes ☐ No	
What is the price?	$_____	$_____	
Does their product look like mine?	☐ a little ☐ just like ☐ not much	☐ a little ☐ just like ☐ not much	
Size: Is theirs . . .	☐ larger ☐ smaller ☐ same size	☐ larger ☐ smaller ☐ same size	
Construction/Quality/Design: Is theirs . . .	☐ better ☐ equal ☐ inferior	☐ better ☐ equal ☐ inferior	
POPULAR MAGAZINE:			
Are there ads selling my product?	☐ Yes ☐ No	☐ Yes ☐ No	
What is the price?	$_____	$_____	
Does their product look like mine?	☐ a little ☐ just like ☐ not much	☐ a little ☐ just like ☐ not much	
Size: Is theirs . . .	☐ larger ☐ smaller ☐ same size	☐ larger ☐ smaller ☐ same size	
Construction/Quality/Design: Is theirs . . .	☐ better ☐ equal ☐ inferior	☐ better ☐ equal ☐ inferior	

valleys in popularity (macramé, sand painting, crochet). Know the current market value of your craft. The more popular your craft is with crafters, the higher the level of competition and the greater the level of expertise you will need. The more popular it is with customers, the higher the price you can charge.

Let's test your knowledge of your craft, its popularity and its market saturation level with another little quiz found on pages 22-23. Use the craft technique you used to make the product in the first quiz to keep the results consistent. Eventually, use the survey for each type of craft you make. Complete the "Before MR" side of the quiz.

How well do you know your craft market? Give yourself 5 points for each correct answer.

☐ Very well (score 80-100)

☐ Just OK (score 60-79)

☐ Not well (score 40-59)

☐ Hardly at all (below 40)

Now *physically* study each one of the selling environments listed. Answer the "After MR" side of the survey. List other questions you could ask to get an even better understanding of your crafts market:

1. _____?

2. _____?

3. _____?

Know Your Customers

Crafters often start out by making a product they eventually find doesn't appeal to their customers. Why? Because they don't know who their customers are, so the products they make somehow miss their mark. If you don't know who your customers are, you can't possibly know where to find them. You might be choosing crafts shows that do not cater at any reasonable level to the customers who would buy your products.

Let's test your knowledge of your customer using the same product you used for our other quizzes. Close your eyes and envision the customer who buy this product. Remember, it's who physically buys it—not whom they buy it for.

At the very next crafts show you participate in, survey your customers using our quiz form on page 24, one for each customer. Average the answers and fill in the "After MR" section of your quiz. Ideally, you should do this for every customer who buys any product from you. How did your perception of your customers compare with reality? Give yourself ten points for each correct answer.

☐ Very well (80-100)

☐ Just OK (70-80)

☐ Not well (60-70)

☐ I don't know them at all (below 60)

There are many more questions to answer about your customers then those given here. What else do you need to know about the people who buy your products? Add the questions to your survey.

1. _____?

2. _____?

3. _____?

You can learn as much (maybe even more) from customers who *don't* buy from you as you can from those who do. In speaking to customers ask questions such as, "Were you looking for anything in particular"? Listen closely to the answers and take notes. Pay attention to the questions they ask you. "Do you have this in red?" "Do you have this in a larger size?" Listen to what they say to their friends as they shop—"I didn't want to spend that much." "I like the one with the lace better than the one with the ruffles." "I wish they had this in a smaller size—I'd get one for my daughter too!" Each question and comment tells you something. You need only to listen.

At the next crafts show you participate in, write down five questions your customers asked you and how you answered them:

1. Q. _____?

   A. _____.

2. Q. _____?

   A. _____.

3. Q. _____?

   A. _____.

4. Q. _____?

   A. _____.

CRAFT:	BEFORE MR *(market research)*	AFTER MR *(market research)*	SCORE
MAJOR DEPARTMENT STORE:			
Does any department in this store focus on products made by my craft method?	☐ Yes ☐ No	☐ Yes ☐ No	
If yes, how many *different* products? If after your market research the answer is "no," give yourself 5 points anyway for not having any competition.	☐ 1–5 ☐ 6–10 ☐ more than 10	☐ 1–5 ☐ 6–10 ☐ more than 10	
GENERAL MERCHANDISE STORE:			
Does any department in this store focus on products made by my craft method?	☐ Yes ☐ No	☐ Yes ☐ No	
If yes, how many *different* products? If after your market research the answer is "no," give yourself 5 points anyway for not having any competition.	☐ 1–5 ☐ 6–10 ☐ more than 10	☐ 1–5 ☐ 6–10 ☐ more than 10	
DISCOUNT STORE:			
Does any department in this store focus on products made by my craft method?	☐ Yes ☐ No	☐ Yes ☐ No	
If yes, how many *different* products? If after your market research the answer is "no," give yourself 5 points anyway for not having any competition.	☐ 1–5 ☐ 6–10 ☐ more than 10	☐ 1–5 ☐ 6–10 ☐ more than 10	
SPECIALTY STORE/GIFT SHOP:			
Does any department in this store focus on products made by my craft method?	☐ Yes ☐ No	☐ Yes ☐ No	
If yes, how many *different* products? If after your market research the answer is "no," give yourself 5 points anyway for not having any competition.	☐ 1–5 ☐ 6–10 ☐ more than 10	☐ 1–5 ☐ 6–10 ☐ more than 10	
MAIL ORDER CATALOG:			
Does any department in this store focus on products made by my craft method?	☐ Yes ☐ No	☐ Yes ☐ No	
If yes, how many *different* products? If after your market research the answer is "no," give yourself 5 points anyway for not having any competition.	☐ 1–5 ☐ 6–10 ☐ more than 10	☐ 1–5 ☐ 6–10 ☐ more than 10	

CRAFT:	BEFORE MR *(market research)*	AFTER MR *(market research)*	SCORE
FLEA MARKET:			
Have I seen booths with products made by my crafts method at the flea market?	☐ Yes ☐ No	☐ Yes ☐ No	
If yes, how many *different* products? If after your market research the answer is "no," give yourself 5 points anyway for not having any competition.	☐ 1–5 ☐ 6–10 ☐ more than 10	☐ 1–5 ☐ 6–10 ☐ more than 10	
HOME SHOPPING NETWORK:			
Are many "handmade" products using my craft made sold on Home Shopping Network?	☐ Yes ☐ No	☐ Yes ☐ No	
If yes, how many *different* products? If after your market research the answer is "no," give yourself 5 points anyway for not having any competition.	☐ 1–5 ☐ 6–10 ☐ more than 10	☐ 1–5 ☐ 6–10 ☐ more than 10	
THE INTERNET:			
Can products made from my craft be purchased on the Internet?	☐ Yes ☐ No	☐ Yes ☐ No	
If yes, how many *different* products? If after your market research the answer is "no," give yourself 5 points anyway for not having any competition.	☐ 1–5 ☐ 6–10 ☐ more than 10	☐ 1–5 ☐ 6–10 ☐ more than 10	
CRAFTS SHOW:			
Are there more than 2 or 3 booths of products made by my crafts method?	☐ Yes ☐ No	☐ Yes ☐ No	
If yes, how many *different* products? If after your market research the answer is "no," give yourself 5 points anyway for not having any competition.	☐ 1–5 ☐ 6–10 ☐ more than 10	☐ 1–5 ☐ 6–10 ☐ more than 10	
CRAFTS MAGAZINE:			
Are products made from my craft method featured in the crafts magazine?	☐ Yes ☐ No	☐ Yes ☐ No	
If yes, how many *different* products? If after your market research the answer is "no," give yourself 5 points anyway for not having any competition.	☐ 1–5 ☐ 6–10 ☐ more than 10	☐ 1–5 ☐ 6–10 ☐ more than 10	

CUSTOMER PROFILE:	BEFORE MR *(market research)*	AFTER MR *(market research)*	SCORE
Gender:	☐ Female ☐ Male	☐ Female ☐ Male	
Age:	☐ Under 12 years old ☐ 13 to 18 years old ☐ 19 to 25 years old ☐ 26 to 40 years old ☐ 41 to 55 years old ☐ over 55 years old	☐ Under 12 years old ☐ 13 to 18 years old ☐ 19 to 25 years old ☐ 26 to 40 years old ☐ 41 to 55 years old ☐ over 55 years old	
Marital Status:	☐ Married ☐ Divorced ☐ Widowed ☐ Single ☐ Cohabitating	☐ Married ☐ Divorced ☐ Widowed ☐ Single ☐ Cohabitating	
Annual Household Income:	☐ Under $15,000 ☐ $15,001 to $25,000 ☐ $25,001 to $39,000 ☐ $39,001 to $50,000 ☐ $50,001 to $75,000 ☐ $75,001 to $100,000 ☐ Over $100,000	☐ Under $15,000 ☐ $15,001 to $25,000 ☐ $25,001 to $39,000 ☐ $39,001 to $50,000 ☐ $50,001 to $75,000 ☐ $75,001 to $100,000 ☐ Over $100,000	
Living Conditions:	☐ Rent ☐ Own	☐ Rent ☐ Own	
Type of Home:	☐ Apartment ☐ House ☐ Condo ☐ Other: _____	☐ Apartment ☐ House ☐ Condo ☐ Other: _____	
Employment Status:	☐ Employed ☐ Self-Employed ☐ Unemployed	☐ Employed ☐ Self-Employed ☐ Unemployed	
Level of Employment:	☐ Part-Time ☐ Full-Time	☐ Part-Time ☐ Full-Time	
Occupation:	☐ Professional ☐ Entrepreneur ☐ White Collar ☐ Blue Collar ☐ Homemaker	☐ Professional ☐ Entrepreneur ☐ White Collar ☐ Blue Collar ☐ Homemaker	
Reason for Purchase:	☐ Personal Use ☐ Gift	☐ Personal Use ☐ Gift	
TOTAL SCORE:			_____

5. Q. _____?

   A. _____.

Write down five questions that you asked your customers—and their answers.

1. Q. _____?

   A. _____.

2. Q. _____?

   A. _____.

3. Q. _____?

   A. _____.

4. Q. _____?

   A. _____.

5. Q. _____?

   A. _____.

List five comments you heard from your customers:

1. _____.

2. _____.

3. _____.

4. _____.

5. _____.

Review these answers and comments over and over until you understand what your customers or potential customers were trying to say to you.

You will no doubt have learned a few things about your product market, your craft market and your customers from taking these quizzes and studying these conversations. That's good. Will you *use* what you have learned to make changes resulting in better and more consistent sales? Or will you continue on as before? The choice is yours.

Drawing Conclusions From Your Market Research

When you conducted your market research did you find your products sold everywhere from flea markets to Macy's? Do you think your product's or your craft's market is saturated? Did your customers want products other than those you sold? Did they or didn't they like products made from your craft?

Whatever the answers to these and other market research questions, don't be discouraged. There is still time and room for you to make adjustments. It's never too late. Once you have identified the problem, you can start to effect the cure. It is only when you don't see the problem that you run into trouble.

Your market research is only as good as the conclusions you draw from it. Most of what you learn will be solid fact. If fifty customers express clearly that they don't like the colors you use, it cannot be disputed. You have used the wrong colors for the market you are selling to. An indisputable conclusion.

Your next question should be, "What do I do about it?" You have two choices here. Whether these same colors will appeal to a different customer group still remains to be seen. You could (1) try selling your product at another crafts show with a different customer base, or (2) change your product's color to suit the market you are currently serving. Perhaps your products will be just the right color for customers at that other show. Maybe your products, in that color, won't sell anywhere. Since you have already made the product, I would try selling it elsewhere before giving up on it altogether.

Some of the conclusions drawn from your market research will be more judgment calls than hard fact. Be careful here. Too many incorrect judgments or conclusions can lead you in a wrong and expensive direction.

Let's assume for a moment your craft is macramé and your product line is macramé wall hangings and plant hangers. In the course of your market research, you have not found this craft/product category at craft shows, in commercial catalogs or anywhere else in the retail market. From this fact you may draw one of the following conclusions: (1) There is a gap in the market and a real need for this product; or (2) Consumers are not interested in purchasing macramé products and that is why no one is selling them. As you can see, these two judgments are very different. The consequences of acting on a bad judgment call can be devastating. By making an incorrect judgment, you might end up developing a whole line of products that would not sell. On the other hand, if you acted on the right conclusion, you would enjoy great sales and an exclusive market.

Take it slowly. If you think a certain change or product could result in great sales, test market first before producing great quantities of product. If the product sells, make more of them. If it sells well, make many more! If it doesn't sell, your judgment was incorrect. Write off the loss, forgive yourself and reanalyze your market research.

Conduct extensive market research—over several months' time at least—before making any major adjustments to your individual products, your product line, your craft, or to whom and where you sell. Research many markets and many selling environments within that market. Ask many questions of as many customers as you can find. The more extensive your market research, the less chance of serious error when drawing your conclusions.

Make each change—even seemingly insignificant ones—slowly, one at a time. Analyze the results of each one on its own merit, before changing anything else. If you make two or three changes at one time, you may not know which one and to what extent each increased your sales. If you make them one at a time, you'll be able to gauge the effectiveness and success of each change.

Somewhere, in the vast crafts marketplace, there is a place for you, your craft and your products—either as they are now, or after a few changes have been made.

Your market research will not only have shown you the competition you face, but, if you look closely and read between the lines, it will also have shown you a few gaps in the same markets where no or few products fill an existing need. These gaps are your ticket to sales success. Look for them. Identify them. Capitalize on them.

For my own product line, I found gaps in the sizes of the tree skirts offered for sale, both commercially and at crafts shows. Average sizes were available everywhere; tiny, small and extra-large products were almost non-existent. This was my ticket to sales success. I found a gap in the market and capitalized on it.

Product, Price and Value

The income you derive from the sale of your crafts products results from assigning correct prices that realistically cover your expenses and allow a reasonable margin of profit. But the price should also reflect both the real and perceived *value* of your products. Today's buyers are more discriminating than ever. They expect *quality* in any product they buy. Let's start with the basics of a successful product and see how yours measures up.

The Basics of a Successful Product

One of the basics of a successful product is to make sure it is "store quality." I always tell new crafters that to make a product store quality, it should be *neat, complete* and *unique*. And though it should look *handmade*, it should not look *homemade*. Stand back and take a critical look at your product. Would it sell in a store environment or would it look primitive and out of place?

Is it neatly finished? There should be no loose threads, no glue showing and no other imperfections but those deliberately designed to enhance its appeal.

Is it complete? Nothing should need to be added to make it immediately usable by your customers. Artwork without a frame or matting, or a jewelry pendant without a chain, are not immediately usable products. They still require the customer to make an additional purchase to have a complete product. Always offer your customer the option to purchase a complete product. It could increase your sales significantly.

Is your product unique? Selling the same products every other crafter is selling will not set you apart in this competitive marketplace. Make it different to give you that much-needed market edge.

Does your product look *handmade* or *homemade*? Make it as professional a piece as you are capable of producing.

But having a neat, complete and even unique handmade product is only the beginning. A product has to be priced correctly to sell consistently. You must take into consideration not only the cost of the product but also its value. Price versus value is an interesting issue.

Pricing Your Products

How you price your products is an integral part of your marketing strategy—and probably the one crafters have the most difficulty with.

If you set your prices too low, your products will probably sell more quickly. But though you may be happy with your *sales* you probably won't be too happy with your *profit*. Selling at low prices often gives the illusion of making money when, in fact, you may be losing money or just breaking even. This will make it difficult for you to meet your financial obligations. You will not have the money to purchase raw materials to make new product. You will be out of funds when it comes time to pay your entry fees for future crafts shows. You will end up with no money, no product *and* no profit.

Pricing your products too low also diminishes the value of your work. "Cheap" is the buzz word for flea markets and "tag" or garage sales where the worn, the old, the unwanted and the recycled are sold at low prices. Since your products do not and should not fit into any of these categories, there is no reason to sell them cheap. Selling at discounted prices is not a viable option for you as a crafter.

Many new crafters set low prices because they are insecure about their creative talents and really have no idea what the customer market will pay for their particular products. I did this myself when I first started selling crafts. But my market research showed my customers would pay more for my products *if* I made the products the way they wanted and needed them made.

While some crafters are shy and humble when it comes to pricing their work, there are others who think they have invented their craft or created another Velcro. Their ego and not their logic reigns when setting prices. Yes, your products have value. Yes, you should expect to be paid well for a product well made. But, no, you cannot expect the consumer to pay for your learning curve nor can you expect them to pay more for a product just because *you* made it.

Setting too high a price will make your products harder to sell. The longer your products remain in inventory, the greater the opportunity for them to become frayed, chipped or broken before they are sold. By overvaluing your products, you might price yourself right out of the very market you set out to conquer.

For new crafters, I offer this piece of advice: Make your products the best you can make them. View your products objectively, not emotionally, and then don't be afraid to go out and ask a price that truly reflects the cost and value of your work. Don't be shy. Don't be humble. But *do* be realistic.

So how do you arrive at just the right price for your products? Well, setting a correct and reasonable price is a delicate balance somewhere between covering your costs, making a good and realistic profit, and not charging more than the market will bear. Let's start with a basic dollars-and-cents approach to calculating your selling price and then we can go on from there.

Basic *wholesale* pricing formula:

Cost of Raw Materials × 2

    plus

Cost of Labor (at $10/hour)

    plus

Cost of Overhead

The resulting figure should be doubled to cover the cost of retail selling.

The Basic Pricing Formula

There is a basic formula most crafters use for calculating the wholesale selling price of a product. Though we are dealing in this book with retail sales (sold directly to the consumer), it all starts with the basic wholesale selling price (used when selling to someone who will *resell* your products, such as a store). Your wholesale selling price should cover all of your production and overhead costs and still provide a good profit margin. That price is then usually doubled to cover the cost of selling retail.

To calculate your wholesale price, start with the cost of the *raw materials* necessary to make the product. Multiply that number by two. If you use very expensive raw materials, multiply the cost by one and a half. If your materials are inexpensive, multiply the cost by three.

Add to that the cost of *labor.* I usually charge $10 an hour for my time. Some crafters charge as much as $15 per hour. If your products are not difficult to make, charge $10. If your craft is a highly skilled one or your product is labor-intensive, pay yourself more per hour.

Then you must figure in your *overhead* expenses. Now, this is where many crafters lose money. They usually underestimate their overhead. Overhead consists of any and all expenses necessary to run your business. This may include postage and phone calls to contact suppliers; fees for licensing, crafts and crafts club memberships; subscriptions to crafts magazines and enrollment fees in crafts workshops and seminars; bank fees and office supplies; utility bill increases due to your crafts business; insurance to safeguard your crafts and reduce your liability; and any other costs directly attributable to your crafts business but *not* to the production of particular product. Overhead is the catchall category.

After you calculate the raw materials costs, your hourly wage and overhead, double that wholesale figure to arrive at a ballpark retail selling price. Doubling your wholesale price for retail selling may seem like overkill, but the difference between retail and wholesale pricing lies in the *cost of selling.* Craft show expenses—show entry fees, display equipment, mileage and gas—are expenses that have to be paid for somehow. By doubling your wholesale price, you should cover these and still leave yourself a nice margin of profit.

These basic pricing formulas will not work for all products and all crafts in all markets, but it is a good, practical starting point. Whatever pricing formula you do use should be closely monitored to make sure it truly does leave you that margin of profit.

Once these accounting factors have been incorporated into the price, the resulting numbers will probably need to be adjusted further. The price of a product should not only reflect its cost, but also its fair market value.

The fair market value *of a product is a combination of its* real *and* perceived *value in today's market.*

Fair Market Value

What exactly is "fair market value"? Market value is what the consumer will actually pay for your product. "Value" is both subjective and objective. In other words, some features that add value to a product are obvious or real while others are implied or perceived and may or may not be real. The more value—both real or perceived, the higher the selling price of the product.

Here's an example. A female customer is looking for a bracelet to buy as a gift for her sister. These are her choices:

1. (Crafter-made) solid 14k yellow gold bracelet ($80)
2. (Tiffany's) hollow sterling silver bracelet ($50)
3. (Discount store) hollow 14k yellow gold bracelet ($40)
4. (Crafter-made) solid sterling silver bracelet ($50)
5. (Jewelry store) solid 14k white gold bracelet ($80)

Let's put design and individual customer taste aside for a moment and assume the bracelets are all similar and the customer likes them all equally. If you were the customer, which one would you choose? Which one would you rather receive as a gift? Which one is the better *value?*

Part of the reason for a customer's preference of one bracelet over another might be due to the price of the product. But the evaluation of price versus value will also be influenced by the product's real value versus the perception of the value of the product.

Real value: 14-karat gold, ounce for ounce, is more valuable than sterling silver. It's a fact that can't be debated. This is how most customers would view the choices. This is probably how the gift recipient would view it also.

Real value: A *solid* bracelet is really more valuable than a *hollow* bracelet made from the same metal. Again, there's no debate here. More metal equals more real value.

Though the real value of a product is difficult to dispute, a customer's *perception* of a product's value can vary greatly. Some examples of perceived value that might alter a customer's choice to purchase might be size, weight, seller or selling location and price.

SIZE

There are some customers who follow the "bigger is better" supposition. The same product in a bigger size should cost more. If one bracelet were larger than the other—even slightly—some customers would choose the larger one just because of its size. On the other hand, there are also customers who follow the "less is more" theory . . .

WEIGHT

On the same premise, a heavier product is often perceived as more valuable than a light one. There must be more of whatever it's made of, therefore it must be more valuable. Even in the case of a hollow gold bracelet versus a solid silver bracelet, a customer might choose the heavier solid rather than the lighter hollow bracelet.

SELLER OR SELLING LOCATION

A customer might prefer spending more money on a silver bracelet just because it is wrapped in a Tiffany box than spending less money on a gold bracelet from a discount or department store.

PRICE

For some, "the very best" is equated only with "the most expensive." They might choose the highest-priced bracelets in either the gold or the silver (depending on their budget) just because it costs more.

COLOR

Though bracelets number one and number five both may have the same amount of gold, the bracelet from the jewelry store is made of white gold, while the crafter's bracelet is made of yellow gold. White is not the "right color" of gold and looks too much like less expensive silver. A customer having to make a choice might opt for the bracelet that is perceived as more expensive, though each has the same *real* value and contains exactly the same amount of gold.

Both perceived and real values can justify charging a higher price for a product. As crafters, this is important. This is where your customer market research is especially helpful. What would make your particular customers see more value in your work? Which bracelet would *your* customers choose?

Anything you can do to your product that will make it seem more special, that will help your customers see value *in it, either perceived or real, will help them justify paying whatever price you are asking for whatever it is you are selling.*

My products, in comparison to their retail counterparts, do have more real value just as yours probably do. The materials I use are more expensive, more interesting and of better quality. That's a fact. The construction and features of my product are superior to those sold in most stores. Because of this, my products will last longer and will need to be replaced less frequently. This is *real* value.

I make sure my customers know the difference between my products and similar ones they can find in stores. That is *marketing*—giving the customer information that will help them justify the sale and validate your higher prices. But don't disappoint your customers either. Turn their perception into reality. Make sure your products are better.

What you have learned from your research will be invaluable in helping you set a current and correct *fair market value* on your products. Your market research should have shown you where your competition lies not only in the world of crafts but also in the common marketplace. You know where similar products are sold and you know how much they are selling for. You have studied the demand factor of your products and know whether they are particularly "hot" right now or just in the mainstream. You are now ready to estimate the fair market value of your products.

Features that add market value:

a) *sign* your pieces

b) *date* your work

c) produce *limited editions*

d) offer a special *series*

e) *name* your products

Here is how I price my products as an example. Christmas tree skirts sell in a general merchandise store for $19 to $39. In a Christmas shop or other specialty store, they sell for anywhere from $39 to $59. I sell mine for $59 to $75, more than twice the price of those sold at the general merchandise store price and about 50 percent more than a Christmas or specialty shop. (Some I even sell for $125.) Now, this may seem very expensive, but it is what my market will bear.

That is why market research should be done *before* you start to sell your crafts. How would you like to sell two hundred pieces of product for a profit of $5 each (total profit $1,000) only to learn later you could have sold that same two hundred pieces for a profit of $10 each (total profit $2,000)? You would have cheated yourself out of $1,000 in clear profit.

Ultimately, whatever the market will bear is what you should sell your products for. If it is far greater than the selling price you initially arrived at, count yourself lucky and enjoy the additional profits. If it is less, then you need to cut your costs to increase your profits. You may have to rethink your production practices, raw material purchases and, in some cases, even your product design to increase your profit. And, in rare cases, perhaps you will need to find a new product to sell, one that makes crafting more profitable. You can't survive in a crafts *business* making a product that doesn't produce a reasonable profit.

Other Ways to Add Value to Your Products

There are many ways to infuse the perception of value into your work. When you do this, you increase the potential to make even more profit on each piece.

SIGNING YOUR WORK

Sign your craft pieces. Put your name or initials on the finished product. If you are proud of your work, then let everyone know who made it.

Let's take a fictitious product line and apply some marketing ideas to add extra value and a "specialness" to the product. Susan Waters, d.b.a. (doing business as) The Holly House, is a crafter of hand-painted original decorative Christmas plates. On the back of each plate, she has inscribed her company name as well as her signature.

THE HOLLY HOUSE
by *Susan Waters*

Doesn't that *sound* special? Wouldn't that *look* special? Immediately, the plate Susan made becomes a little more important and valuable because the artisan has taken the time to sign it.

Depending on the products you make, you might not want to sign every piece, but do sign your top-of-the-line or higher-priced products. This will give them an air of exclusivity. It will set them apart from other products in your product line and justify a higher price.

DATING YOUR WORK

You might also want to add the date or year in which you created the product to your inscription. Susan puts out a new Christmas plate each year. The back of the plate might read . . .

THE HOLLY HOUSE
by *Susan Waters*
1997

This is usually a positive feature but sometimes it may work against you. If you have created a product that has stayed on the shelf too long, this will become very evident to the consumer if the product is dated. On the other hand, it is a wise practice to always carry some prior years' editions so a new collector can purchase back issues and complete the set.

NUMBERED LIMITED EDITIONS

Some crafters go even further than just signing or dating their work. They may offer a "limited edition" product. When producing a limited edition piece, the crafter only makes a certain number of pieces of that product and consecutively numbers each piece. It is understood that no more of that product in that particular design will be made once the original number have been sold.

THE HOLLY HOUSE
by *Susan Waters*
#102 of 250

Now, this is not to say you could not make that same product with a different design—you could. But no more pieces identical to the original product should be made. This is the commitment you make when you label a product "limited edition" and number your pieces. Your customer is buying a product of which only 250 pieces exist in the world. The next edition should contain substantial differences from the original.

Perhaps you produce one piece—the pride and joy of your product line—that requires a great deal more time and work than your other pieces. You cannot mass-produce it even at a crafter level. Yet this product is an integral part of your product line and a real showstopper. You can't possibly price it at the same level as your other products. You need to ask a higher price to make it profitable to continue producing this piece. What could you do to justify making and selling this piece? You could offer it as a limited edition, selling fewer pieces, but charging more for each piece.

SPECIAL SERIES PIECES

You may also choose to offer a special *series* of products. In this case, there would be several different designs in the series but they would all contain a common thread linking them together. The series pieces could be produced in numbered limited editions or not as you choose.

THE HOLLY HOUSE
"The Night Before Christmas" Series
by *Susan Waters*

Producing a special series of products is a great way to ensure repeat business. If the series appeals to your customers, they may want to collect all of the pieces. This will go a long way toward increasing your sales.

GIVING PRODUCTS NAMES AND TITLES

It is also a nice touch to give your individual products or special series pieces *names* so they are easily recognized and a customer can order them by name. If you make dolls, you might want to name them "Melissa," "Prudence," "Butch" and so on—each with its own distinctive attitude reflected in your choice of names. Or you could give them *titles* such as "Little Miss Sunshine" and "Little Miss Mischief" and call the whole series the "Little Miss" series.

For jewelry, all products—earrings, bracelets, necklaces and rings having the same design—might be called "Simplicity" while a more bold and brassy design might be named "Pizzazz." You could name your jewelry sets after famous people—"The Jackie O" collection . . . the "Garbo," etc. If a customer purchases one piece, they could call you at any time and order additional pieces of the set by name.

Susan's Christmas plates might read . . .

THE HOLLY HOUSE
The Night Before Christmas Series
"The Meaning of Christmas"
by *Susan Waters*

THE HOLLY HOUSE
The Night Before Christmas Series
"The Sleepiest Little Angel"
by *Susan Waters*

There are also more subtle ways to convey the value of your products. Just by mentioning a piece is an "original design" will make your customers look twice at it.

When selling my Christmas tree skirts, I always mention that I purchase only the finest fabrics and that my products are well made and "heirloom quality." A handy bit of information for my customers to know.

For my more labor-intensive products, I describe to customers the creation and manufacturing process of those pieces. When I get through, there isn't one customer who would dare say, "Oh, *I* could make that!" They realize it would be much easier to just *buy* the product from me. Suddenly, the price of the product doesn't seem quite so high. An informed customer will be your best customer. Give them what they need to justify the purchase—information. Give them a reason to buy.

All of these strategies add greater market value to your products and lend an air of importance to your whole product line. They may make your pieces "collectibles." They may help your customers remember your products, increasing the chance for future purchases. Use these features for your very special, expensive or hardest-to-produce pieces or use them all—in different combinations—for your entire product line.

Positioning Your Product

How do you arrive at just the *right* price for your products after you have factored in all of the actual and perceived variables? Where should your product fit into the market of other similar products?

Well, first you need to answer some questions. Do you want to offer the *best* and *most expensive* version of the product? I wouldn't recommend it. It would be very hard to sell in today's economy. Do you want to offer an *economy* version of the product? One that is scaled down but still does the job? Not a good choice. Customers come to crafts shows to buy *better* product.

I would say that your product should fit in on the high side of the middle of your particular product/craft market. After you have examined your market research information and determined (a) what the discount versions are going for, (b) what the average price of your product is in today's market, and (c) what the most expensive competition is charging, calculate the difference in price between the most expensive and the average version of your product. Split that number in half. That is where your products should probably fit in.

If the discounted version of your product sells for $15, the average price is $30 and the expensive versions sell for $45, your product and your price should be around $35 to $40. Now, as with any pricing rule, this is not written in stone. Try it and see if it works for your products.

Ultimately, your goal is to find your product, price and value niche within the current market—where your product will sell *best*. A price at which you can sell product within a reasonable amount of time. A price your particular customers can comfortably afford and feel they have received value for their money. A price that produces a large enough profit margin for you to be comfortable.

This might take a little time. Don't think you will just pick a price (even after a well thought-out market-research study) and come up with the "perfect" price for your products. Often, it takes a little trial and error before you arrive at a price that provides the most profit and still allows the most sales. But it can be done.

PRICE COMPARISON STUDY

Product _____

Price Parameters of similar products:

CHEAPEST VERSIONS

Selling Price Range: $ _____ to $_____

Features its has: 1) _____

2) _____

3) _____

Features it lacks: 1) _____

2) _____

3) _____

MODERATE VERSIONS

Selling Price Range: $ _____ to $_____

Features it has: 1) _____

2) _____

3) _____

Features it lacks: 1) _____

2) _____

3) _____

EXPENSIVE VERSIONS

Selling Price Range: $ _____ to $_____

Features it has: 1) _____

2) _____

3) _____

Features it lacks: 1) _____

2) _____

3) _____

MY PRODUCT

Selling Price Range: $ _____ to $_____

Features it has: 1) _____

2) _____

3) _____

Features it lacks: 1) _____

2) _____

3) _____

Marketing Your Business

J ust because you sell crafts and not commercial merchandise or services doesn't mean you can afford to ignore the fundamentals of good advertising and effective promotion for your *business* as well as your products. Crafting a professional image will give your business credibility. Market your business as you would your products—aggressively and professionally.

To do this, you need professional-looking business literature—business cards, letterhead, order forms, separate imprinted checks and a few other things that will help people take your business seriously. But first, we need to decide what will be printed on this literature, starting with the name of your company.

Your Company Name

Your crafts company name should embody the very nature of your business—a name easily remembered, catchy but not too cute to be taken seriously. A name your customer can identify with you, your products and your craft. It should tell your customers something about your company. "Speedy Dry Cleaners" says *what* about that company? It tells you the nature of the business (dry cleaning) as well as what makes the company *special* (quick service).

A complete *business* image package should consist of your company name and logo on:

- business cards
- letterhead and envelopes
- order forms and sell sheets
- product packaging
- business checking account

If you already have a company name, ask yourself, "If I had to do it all over again, would I choose the same name?" If the answer is "no," and you and your crafts company have not reached a reasonable level of recognition and popularity, now is the time to rethink the name—before you go any further.

What, exactly, do you *do* (craft)? What do you *make* (products)? What is *special* about your company and your crafts? What do you want your customers to know (remember) about your crafts company? What features do you want to stress? The answers to all of these questions should be taken into consideration when choosing a name.

Don't make your company name too long. It should fit comfortably on your business card. You don't want it to have to be abbreviated to accommodate someone's computer database file. Sometimes very long names are catchy—"The Most Incredible Toys Your Child Will Ever Own" company—but they can still be difficult to remember. Short and sweet is better in most cases.

Don't make the name too vague. "Lovely Creations" as the name of a crafts business selling florals would be a waste of advertising space where the company name might appear. It conveys no meaningful information. But don't go to the other extreme with too descriptive a title either. Use as few words as possible while still getting your meaning across.

A very dear friend of mine, Kris Gould, makes silver and gold jewelry. She has named her business "Silver & Gould." Short and sweet; clever and catchy. It tells you *what* she makes and *who* makes it—all in three little words.

Here are some other ways to make your company name more memorable:

- Make it *rhyme*: "Crazy Daisies"
- Incorporate your *name* into the title: "Morrison Handcrafted Toys"
- Use *alliteration*: "Tiny Tot Toys"
- Use a *combination* of alliteration, rhyme and/or your name: "Kit's Knits" or "Kit's Krazy Knits"
- Incorporate a *familiar phrase*: " 'Tis the Season—for Christmas Crafts, "All That Glitters—for a line of gold products
- Play on words: "Faux Ever Wood"—Faux-finished wood pieces
- Whimsical: "Ooglies"—ugly but lovable dolls, "Quackers"—comical duck figurines
- Make it *clever*: "Eggstraordinaries"—crafts made from real eggs, "Quinn's Quazy Quilts"
- Use the *obvious*: "Tic Tock Clocks"
- Impart *information*: "Fred the Fudge Man," "Tiki Polychromatic Tableware"
- The *unusual*: "The Iron Maiden"—a woman crafter selling iron products
- *Anything*: so your customers won't forget your company's name and will associate it with your products. Give it personality! Give it pizzazz!

A Company Logo

"A picture is worth a thousand words." Many businesses use a company logo to attach a visual image to their company concept. The logo is used in conjunction with the company name to reinforce the message. In some cases, the logo becomes so recognizable that by the logo alone, you automatically know which company it is. A memorable *image* is built around the business and this image is reinforced on absolutely every piece of printed matter having to do with the company and its products—business cards, price tags, packaging, sales literature, advertising and even on the product itself.

If your crafts company becomes very successful and your name and logo well known, you might even want to have it trademarked so no one else can use it. But registering a trademark is an expensive undertaking costing thousands of dollars. You will have to weigh the cost against the risk of someone else usurping it.

Business Cards

All too often, crafters try to save money by cutting down on what they feel are superfluous advertising or promotional expenses such as business cards. This is a grave error in judgment. Printed business cards are cheap when you weigh the cost against the amount of business they can generate. Business cards are effective sales tools that pay for themselves over and over again. Don't go to a show without them.

Your business cards should include all the necessary information for customers to be able to contact you—name, company name, mailing address, telephone number, as well as other information to help them remember you, such as a description of product and craft, and company logo.

If you choose not to include your address on your business cards, then a post office box number should be substituted. Not only will customers be picking up your business cards for future contact, but scouts for other crafts shows might use your business card data to send your information on their shows.

 Business cards should include the following information:
- your company name
- your name
- company logo
- mailing address (with ZIP code)
- description of product
- telephone number

Creative Business Cards

Boring black-print-on-white-paper business cards are really not in harmony with the image you are trying to convey. After all, you *are* a crafter.

Your business cards should be creative and personal to your products and craft. If your craft is woodworking, perhaps your business card background could be wood-grained to further convey the wood theme. If you sell teddy bears, consider spending the extra money to print a fuzzy flock teddy bear on your business card. For Kris Gould and her "Silver & Gould," the "Silver" in her company name could be embossed in silver; the "Gould embossed in gold, further emphasizing the nature of her crafts.

Phone (444) 931-5671	Fax (444) 931-5562
	Ted the Toymaker
	Wooden Toys for All Ages
(photo here)	1937 East 42nd St., New Hyde, PA 11443

Business cards containing color photographs of your products will help the customer remember your products long after the crafts show ends. These can be ordered from most photo processing centers. Make sure the photographs you submit are clear, in focus and uncluttered. The format is usually similar to this one, but you can also have a larger group photograph on the front of the card and your company information printed on the back.

You can go one step further and even have color product photographs printed directly on your business cards along with the print information. I have found this to be a very effective means of advertising my own products. Your business cards can be backed with magnets for customers to attach to their refrigerators or printed on Rolodex card stock for your customer to file away for future reference. A printer can do either or you could do it yourself—the supplies are available at any office supply store.

With the help of a little clip-art or drawing skills, some imagination, a computer and a color printer, you can easily design your own unique business cards. This may seem time-consuming, but once you have settled on a design that embodies your company image, you have only to save your original creation on a computer disk for easy retrieval. If you don't have a computer, consider a design that be reproduced on a color copier or by using a custom-made rubber stamp.

Business cards are an integral part of your marketing campaign. Don't leave home without them.

Letterhead

Letterhead is a simple and easy way to add a bit of image to your business. Sending a company letter on cute store-bought stationery is not very professional. Create your own stationery on your home computer or have it professionally designed and printed.

When buying wholesale, you will be writing companies for copies of their wholesale catalogs. You will be requesting show schedules from show producers. You will, from time to time, be writing to your customers to answer a question or solve a problem. Letterhead comes in handy.

Product Order Forms

This is another area where most crafters don't bother to venture. Customers don't always make a decision to buy your products at the crafts shows. Some may take an order form home and call you later or send it to you in the mail. You can also send order forms periodically to prior customers—at Christmas time, etc. Even if they don't see you at a show, they can still place an order. You are missing a tremendous sales opportunity by not having these handouts available to your customers.

Professionally printed order forms are expensive, especially if they contain color product photographs. But did you know you can have 1,000 to 2,500 professionally printed for only $250 to $750?

Below are listed some companies that specialize in color photograph printing for order forms, photo business cards and the like. Note: There is a small additional one-time setup or color separation fee for the photograph. Take one group photo of your products rather than separate photos of each product. It will be cheaper that way.

American Color Printing, Inc.
1731 N.W. 97 Avenue
Plantation, FL 33322
Phone: (305) 473-4392
Fax: (305) 473-8621

Color NOW!
1115 West 190th Street
Gardena, CA 90248
Phone: (800) 257-4968
Fax: (310) 327-9598

U.S. PRESS

P.O. Box 640

Valdosta, GA 31603-0640

Phone: (800) 227-7377

Challenge Graphics Services

18 Connor Lane

Deer Park, NY 11729

Phone: (800) 242-5364

Fax: (800) 898-3729

In NY State (516) 586-0171

Color Direct

72 Cascade Dr. Suite 4S

Rochester, NY 14614

Phone: (800) 838-9877

RAPIDCOLOR

705 East Union Street

West Chester, PA 19382

Phone: (800) 872-7436

ProColor Marketing Inc

4715 Christman Rd.

Akron, OH 44319

Phone: (800) 636-3555

Fax: (216) 896-3780

Product Labeling and Packaging

Your goal is to offer a complete *image* package to your customer. Your company name and logo should carry over into everything that has to do with you and your business. Your product price tags, labels, order forms, boxes and bags should all reinforce the message and carry over the *flavor* of your crafts business.

Again, these items don't have to be professionally printed. There are many ways to customize standard materials. One way is to buy or make plain labels and use a custom rubber stamp or computer imaging to emboss your labels, boxes, bags and price tags.

Some products might look better with stock labels and price tags but I, personally, think you should add *personality* to your product presentation. It's often the little things that make one crafter's products stand out over another's.

So use stock price tags and labels if you must, but I would prefer artwork or a uniquely shaped product label over plain white stock any day.

You are playing "connect the dots" here—all the different image-building components of your crafts business *connected* to reinforce your message.

Product packaging need not be expensive, but remember your customer will carry purchases through the crafts show. Other customers will see them. This is *free advertising*. Dolls in boxes with see-through panels, clear bags or packaging with prominently displayed company names, logos and other information could bring you additional business.

All of the image-building components of your crafts business should contain a common thread that can be easily identified. We are playing "connect the dots" here. Business cards, order forms, letterhead and product labeling and packaging should carry the same design to reinforce your message.

Your Business Checking Account

A separate business checking account with your company name printed on your checks adds credibility and reinforces your image as a *business*. It says you're serious and professional.

When you pay for raw materials, apply to a crafts shows, apply for membership in a crafts organization—anything having to do with your crafts business—it is an asset to pay for it by company check.

To be admitted to seminars, wholesale shows and other industry events, you often need proof you are a member of the crafts community. Paying by (or showing) a company check can be one form of acceptable proof.

Credit Card Acceptance

If you really want your sales and crafts business to grow, you must be able to accept major credit cards as a form of payment. There's some paperwork involved, and you have to pay anywhere from 2.5 percent to 5 percent for this service, but it is well worth the time and service fee.

Your customers will be pleased and impressed that you can accept their credit cards. It will build a stronger image of you as a professional. With the influx of home shopping networks, the Internet and the popularity of mail-order shopping, we crafters need to contemporize the way we do business to stay competitive. Credit card acceptance is just another way to do this.

Call directory assistance for the ''merchant information'' telephone number for Visa, MasterCard, Discover Card and American Express right now. It will take a few days or weeks to process the forms before you can become an authorized merchant. Don't procrastinate. At your very next show your sales could increase by 25 percent!

All of these individual components, put together in a professional manner, cannot help but increase the public's perception of you as a professional and serious crafter. Because you obviously take it seriously, they will too. *Image* is worth its weight in gold.

Marketing Yourself

Building Your Image as a Crafter

You, personally, are as much a commodity as the crafts you sell. It's a package deal. When your customers look at you, your business, your products and your presentation, what will they see? What interesting information can you impart about yourself to make your products more appealing to customers? Information that will boost their confidence in your craftsmanship and experience? That may *persuade* them to buy your products?

What makes you able to do the crafts work that you do? What sets you apart from the other crafters in the field? What training have you had? How long have you been making crafts? Developing your technique? Is there information you would like to share with your customers to make them feel they're buying unique merchandise from a crafting professional?

Now, don't be intimidated if you are a new crafter without an extensive track record. That's okay. We all have to start somewhere. At this point in time there may be *nothing* you can say about yourself that would impress your customers. You may not yet have developed a "crafter résumé" of impressive credentials, but you should keep these questions in mind.

Opportunities will arise—they always do—for you to show what you know. The longer you have been in the crafts business, the more experience you will gain. Take advantage of any and every opportunity to add to your prestige as a crafter. Add each experience to your crafter résumé.

Reputation, Publicity and Exposure

Cultivating and expanding your good reputation in the crafts world will go a long way toward increasing your sales. Using the media to *publicize* yourself and your crafts business will add weight to your credibility. Positive public exposure could very well make yours a local household name.

Reputation

Customers will not only remember your products, they will remember *you*. Guard your good reputation. It is a precious commodity difficult to regain once lost. Be pleasant. Always treat people fairly and honestly. Produce a quality product. Stand behind your product. Exchange and repair as necessary. Act in a professional manner. Build a positive image of yourself. Build a good reputation, and you will build a successful crafts business.

Word of mouth is a powerful tool. I always cringe when I hear one customer say to another, "That crafter was actually rude!" And I have heard this. Good news travels fast, but bad news travels even faster. Negative responses and negative attitudes have no place at any time in any selling environment. Every person attending the show is a potential customer. No matter what happens between you and the buying public, always leave your customers on a positive note, even if they didn't buy anything. They may another time. Even if they made a rude comment, don't stoop to their level. Speak nicely and politely to your customers. You need these people.

Show producers don't like to deal with ill-tempered crafters either. They realize even one negative incident can affect the reputation of their whole show. And, frankly, they have enough to worry about without having to deal with a cranky vendor. So, if you gain a reputation for being difficult, you may find your show applications rejected more than they will be accepted. No one wants a party pooper at the party.

Your sales will benefit from your good reputation. Your fellow crafters will respect you for it. Customers will remember you and buy your products with confidence. Crafts shows themselves will benefit just by having you participate. The crafts industry will also profit from your personal reputation and your good-will attitude.

Publicity

Nothing boosts a crafter's image better than some publicity—so put yourself in the spotlight! It's easy to do and you deserve it. But please remember the purpose of publicity is not to inflate your *ego* but to bolster your *image*. Don't let it go to your head.

Print publicity in small local newspapers is the easiest to obtain. And you would be amazed at the increase in business generated by having your face appear in your local newspaper along with a small article about your business. People will recognize you. They will *remember* you.

So, don't waste another minute. Start with your hometown paper. Prepare a script of information about yourself and your business—write about how you got started, about what makes your products special, about something important and something interesting. Include how you can be contacted and where your business is located.

Call your local newspaper and speak with a reporter who handles local news. Tell them about yourself. Use your script as a guide but *don't* read from it. Make it a friendly and informative conversation. Be excited. Be pleasant. Mention *local* shows you have participated in and anywhere you will participate in the near future. Suggest the reporter visit you, take some photographs and perhaps do a feature article on you and your business. It never hurts to ask. The smaller and more local the newspaper, the better the chance they will say yes. Even an article in a hometown newspaper can generate substantial business.

Once one newspaper has written about you, it will be easier to get others. Broaden the base and call newspapers in surrounding towns. Build on prior publicity. Don't let it go to waste or be a one-shot deal. Space your requests at reasonable intervals. If an article was written about you this week in your local town newspaper, the large city newspaper won't want to write another article about you next week. Wait a month, but don't forget about it.

Don't limit your publicity to local media either. National magazines are another way to gain publicity. Though they may not directly increase your sales, they will definitely bolster your image. If *Home Business* magazine or *Crafts* magazine wrote an article about you and your crafts business, you may get some calls and even make a few sales. But even if you don't, just the fact that you appeared in a national publication is significant. Add it to your résumé.

Read and research absolutely every magazine that might possibly consider writing an article about you and your crafts business. Scout them for articles on other crafters. Find out the name of the editor who handles these articles. Call and ask what you need to send them.

Exposure

Media publicity increases your value and expands your résumé. But craft show exposure is key to your more immediate success. Participating in only two or three craft shows a year would not be considered exposing yourself to the public. You need to be constantly and consistently seen for customers to remember you. They will look for your booth when they go to craft shows. They will tell others about you. Your business will grow.

Many crafters only sell during the holiday season—from September to December—when sales are at their peak and the public is in a buying frenzy. It's true this may be your most profitable time of year, but remember you are building your image. It cannot be built in a few short months. Even if you sell seasonal products, extend your show schedule to include shows a few months before your selling season actually begins. It *will* make a difference in your sales.

I once participated in a horrible crafts show in 100° July heat—selling Christmas products. Actually, I was doing it as a favor for a friend who was a member of the nonprofit group sponsoring the show. There weren't many customers at the show. I considered it a flop—until December rolled around and one of the customers from that show called and placed a very large order. Then a friend of hers called and placed another substantial order. You cannot always immediately judge whether or not a show has been successful for you. It is not only the sales on the day of the show, but also the sales resulting from that show that determine its success.

At a Christmas show in December, a customer said, "I saw you at a show in August and I just *loved* these but I couldn't afford to buy at the time. I'm so glad I saw you again. I'll take this one." She bought a $125 Christmas tree skirt.

Another customer at a different show said, "Wasn't there an article written about you in the newspaper a few weeks ago?" She also bought something.

I know many successful crafters whose customers follow them from show to show. Their excellent sales result from a combination of a good *reputation*, media *publicity* and constant, consistent public *exposure*.

Learn Your Craft

Take every opportunity to advance your knowledge of your craft. You can never learn enough. New materials and techniques are always being developed. You don't want to be left behind. Take a class or two at a local college or apprentice with a seasonal professional, then add the experience to your résumé. Experiment with new products, develop new techniques. Then use what you have learned to further your crafter image. If you receive any sort of certificate of completion from any learning experience involving crafts, be sure to add the information to your résumé.

Teach Your Craft

Once you have gained some experience and knowledge in your craft, consider holding craft classes of your own. Many colleges, adult education programs and local craft stores offer craft classes. Even a local school might want to adopt one of your products or techniques for their arts and crafts program.

Call them and offer your services. If you do teach crafts, record the event with photos you can use later for print articles in your local newspaper. Add the experience to your résumé. After the class is over, ask the organizer for a letter of recommendation—that says how wonderful your class was.

Demonstrate Your Craft Expertise

If yours is a craft that can be easily demonstrated, take every opportunity to do so. Volunteer at state, local and county fairs. Demonstrate at craft shows. Some crafts co-ops actually require you to demonstrate your craft on a rotating basis with other crafters in the same co-op. Show them what you know. Take photographs and add these experiences to your crafter résumé.

Demonstrating your crafts on television is also not an impossible feat, especially if you make decorative home products that seem to be the focus of most TV crafts shows. There are many national and local TV crafts shows just begging for new show ideas and new crafts material. If they have been on the air for a while, they are probably running out of ideas.

Watch each TV show for about a month. Get a feel for the show's content. Each has its own underlying agenda. Call the station about submitting an idea. Surprise! You could be on TV! After the show, ask for a copy of the videotape. Take it to a photographic studio and have them take one frame from the video—of you together with the show hosts— and make it into a still photo. Add it to your résumé. Display it in your show booth.

Write About Your Craft

You would be surprised at how many companies would be interested in knowing what you know about the products you make and the craft techniques you use. Not only are you equipped to teach your craft, you may well be in a position to *write* about it as an authority.

Craft and women's magazines may be interested. Book publishers specializing in crafts books might pay you handsomely for what you know. Craft product manufacturers might also pay to learn your techniques and use your finished products, made from their products for "how to" booklets, sales literature and promotional pieces. Just think how that would look on your crafter résumé!

"Trade Secrets"

Some crafters are afraid to show and tell. Let's face it—there really aren't many crafts or craft techniques that are a "secret." If you have one, you should patent it or perhaps license it to an established crafts manufacturer who could mass-produce and sell it for you. And if you have an original product with high mass-market potential, what are you doing at crafts shows? Copyright it, mass-produce it and sell it nationwide.

Otherwise, it's OK to share information. Don't assume that at the next crafts show you attend there will be twenty booths making your product or using your technique. That's highly unlikely. You won't lose your edge by demonstrating one product or one craft technique. But in doing so, you are trading a little bit of information for a far greater increase in your commercial value.

Spreading the Word

Publicity and exposure, no matter what form they take, are image-building tools with a time clock on them. Fame is fleeting. The public has short-term memory. To get the most mileage from your experiences, record each in a tangible form. Take photographs of each and every situation that might prove valuable as part of your résumé. Make copies of them or order extra copies from the photo developer. Never give the originals to anyone. Keep them in your files.

Save and copy newspaper clippings about you, your business and your crafts. Keep a copy of the adult education curriculum program with the class you taught and your name on it. Save a copy of the newspaper ad, flyer or poster when you taught a class at your local crafts shop. Put all of these in a nice binder or art portfolio. Exhibit it at crafts shows. Send copies to show producers with your show application. Tell them about your accomplishments.

Over the course of the last ten years, I have had many newspaper articles written about me, my products and my business. I have also been on national TV and have written books about crafting and the crafts industry. Each of these has added credence to my image as a crafter and as a minor authority on things having to do with crafts. Image is a matter of *perception* as much as reality. And because I have created a substantial image for myself, my *value* has increased.

Recently, in a national crafts magazine, I ran across the name of a fellow crafter I know well—just an average crafter. I also saw several feature articles written about her in a local newspaper and a larger city paper. Whether or not she makes the "best" product is not the issue; it's that her name is plastered over local and national media.

When this crafter applies to a show, rest assured she lets the show producer know just how well the media—national and local—has received her. Don't you think the show producer, having "proof" of this crafter's "success" and "popularity," will give her application special attention? Wouldn't you? And when this crafter exposes her buying public to this information at a crafts show, don't you think they will look twice at her products?

Never underestimate the power and value of publicity and public exposure. It can ultimately be measured in sales dollars. Build your image, and you will build your crafts business as well.

MY CRAFTER RÉSUMÉ

I have been crafting for _____ years, from 19_____ to present.

How I learned my craft:

_____

_____

_____

_____

Craft classes I have attended and instruction I have received:

1. _____

2. _____

3. _____

Credentials and Certificates I have been awarded:

1. _____

2. _____

3. _____

Craft classes I have taught:

Location	Title of Class	Dates

MY CRAFTER RÉSUMÉ *(continued)*

Newspaper articles written about me, my products or my business:

Newspaper	Date	Page Number

I have demonstrated my craft at:

Location/Event	Date

Published works:

Publication	Type of Publicity	Issue

Other points of interest:

1. _____

2. _____

3. _____

Part Two

HOW TO DISPLAY

YOUR CRAFTS

Features of an Effective Crafts Show Display

Participating in crafts shows is an excellent way to show and sell your crafts. It is the avenue most new crafters use to reach their buying public. At a crafts show, you will meet and greet your customers personally. You will learn first-hand about their preferences and you will be able to watch their reactions to the products you sell.

When a customer comes to a crafts show, the first thing they will see is your display—long before they get close enough to focus on your individual products. Your display should be as eye-catching, inviting and appealing as the products it contains. It is as much a reflection of your artistry as the products you sell.

As your profit from your crafts, reinvest some of those profits back into your business in the form of better and more professional display equipment. The right equipment can increase your sales and make selling a whole lot easier.

You will probably try many different materials and display arrangements before you settle on just the right combination. Gradually, the right display for your products will evolve. Take your time. Build your display s-l-o-w-l-y. Consider each new addition carefully before making the purchase. Think of symmetry and harmony.

Display equipment doesn't have to be expensive to be effective. If you know anything about woodworking or have a friend who can wield a hammer, you can make your own display easily and simply. Some flat boards and a few two-by-fours may be all you need to make a *perfect* display for your products.

Often, you can utilize premade products found at general merchandise, hardware, lumber and home improvement stores to make just as handsome a display as any sold by professional display companies. You can also find some charming and reasonably priced equipment at flea markets and yard sales. These will make your display look less commercial and give it more personality and ambience.

Keep in mind a few basics when designing your craft show display. First of all, it should not just *display* your crafts, it should *showcase* them. And your display should be customer-friendly, as well as convenient for you, the crafter. For interest and best use of space, display your crafts on more than one level, using *air* space as well as *floor* space. And since not all crafts show spaces are created equal, you should be able to adapt your display to different show booth dimensions. It must be flexible. The display components should be light, compact and portable so you can easily transport them from show to show. They should also be stable and sturdy to protect your products.

Since you are putting so much effort into your display, make sure you have enough product to fill it. Stock a large selection of inventory. And the final requirement of an effective display is to add personality and ambience.

An effective crafts show display should:
1. *showcase* your particular product and craft
2. be crafter- and customer-*friendly*
3. be *multilevel*
4. be *flexible*
5. be *portable*
6. be *sturdy* and *stable*
7. be *stocked* with sufficient product
8. have *personality* and *ambience*

Now, this might seem like a tall order, but don't you just love a creative challenge? Let's look at each feature individually. Things always seem less daunting that way.

Showcasing Your Crafts

Think of your show booth as fine artwork. Your display equipment is the frame; your crafts are the painting itself. The frame should somehow reflect the flavor of the painting. The size of the frame should fit the painting and allow it to be seen in its entirety. Would you display your painting flat on a table? Silly question. You would display it upright, either on a wall or an easel so everyone could see it. Would you hang it at eye level or belt level? Eye-level, of course. The answers to these questions seem foolishly obvious, don't they? But it you substitute "display" for frame and "crafts" for painting, you will have the answers to the question, "What is the best way to showcase my crafts?"

Showcase your products as they are meant to be used. Hang clothing, accessories, artwork, wall florals and any other product meant to be hung or draped. Exhibit jewelry on body parts—hands, wrist and neck forms—as they are to be worn. If your products are meant to be filled with something (such as baskets and flower pots) by all means fill them with something—not all of them, but definitely some of them—to show the varied uses of your product and to stimulate your customer's own imagination. Put exemplary pieces of your products at eye level in a special setting to really show them off. If you make tableware, set up a small dinner table, complete with napkins, flatware, placemats and a tablecloth to show how your products will look. Frame and group similar products together to make them stand out.

Your crafts show display should also provide optimum product visibility. Customers cannot buy what they cannot see. Don't block your products and display in any way. Leave customers a clear path of vision that will lead them to your products.

Angle your display and your products toward the customer whenever possible. Walk down the show aisle in the direction of your booth, and see how you can position your products and display so they will grab your customer's attention. If you can, set the side pieces of your display at a slight angle, splaying them outwards toward your customers rather than perpendicular to their field of vision. This not only makes your products more visible but is a silent invitation for your customers to "come on in."

A simple step design can elevate your products, making those in the background as visible as those in the foreground. This can be accomplished by designing a special graduated wooden platform on which to place your products or by stacking product storage boxes or shelving in a stair-step configuration. Cover the platform, boxes or shelves with fabrics.

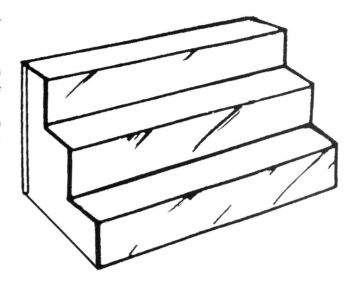

Crafter- and Customer-Friendly

Your customers will want to *touch, hold* and *try on* your products. Make your products accessible to your customers. Many of them will not want to draw attention to themselves until after they have had a closer look at your products (and your prices).

If your products are not easily accessible, your customer might miss the chance to see just how heavy and substantial they are; how fuzzy and soft they feel; how comfortable they might be; how brightly they sparkle

This crafter has a nice presentation but the interior side walls of the display should have been angled more toward her customers, who cannot see what is on the side walls.

A bird's-eye view of this crafter's display.

The same display, with the side walls set at an outward angle toward the customer, makes products more visible and invites customers to "come on in." Angle your display toward your customers whenever space allows.

when you move them in the light; how smooth the wood is finished. Get the idea? Give your customers the opportunity to find out for themselves. Let them come close enough to see (and feel) the detail of every piece. It will make them want to buy it.

And when you design your display, don't forget to provide your customers with a wide enough entrance to your show booth. One that says "Welcome! Come on in!" and not "Come in if you can fit through this opening." Use your show space wisely. Don't overload it with so much display equipment that customers can't move about freely to view your products. Make your customers as comfortable as possible.

Your customers will only be in your show booth for a few minutes while you, on the other hand, will be at your booth all day and, depending on the duration of the show, possibly for several days. Design your booth so you have easy access to everything you need to make and complete a sale. Designate a small area within your show space as your sales area. Equip it with a cash box, pens and pencils, tape, business cards, packaging materials, sales slips, credit card processing equipment, extra price tags—anything and everything you might need.

Having everything in one place will help you close a sale quickly. It will allow you to move on to the next customer sooner. You won't become flustered. You won't end up wading through boxes looking for the tape or sales slip pad. And your customers won't get tired of waiting for you to get organized.

Height and Composition

Design a multilevel display that challenges your customer's eye to take in all that you are offering. Flat, unilevel displays are boring displays. Put some highs and lows into your booth to make it more interesting. Use several different planes to showcase your work. The customer's eyes will be challenged to look from one level to another. They will be forced to focus on the variety of different items you have for sale.

Adding height to your display will also allow you to accommodate more product and enable you to make more money. A large and varied product selection will ensure good sales. You can accommodate five times as much product if you add height to your display. Use air space and not just floor space. Most crafts shows allow a ceiling of six feet for displays. Show booth fees are expensive. Make the most of the space you are given. Use it all.

If you display your product on a low plane or only at table level, you will also be giving your customers the opportunity to look up, over and through your presentation to surrounding displays and products. You don't want to do this. Do everything possible to ensure their attention is focused on *your* products while they are in *your* booth.

This point was reinforced just recently when I went to a local crafts show. As I stood at the first booth and talked with the artisan, my attention was drawn to some interesting artwork two booths away. Without even thinking, I went right past the second crafts booth and on to the third—

This crafter has used her show space wisely, employing interesting wooden crates to build walls that separate her booth from those of other crafters. This product is shown on an upward scale of several different planes, starting with clusters of dolls displayed in charming hat boxes set at ground level.

to the artwork I had seen at a distance. After I left the show, it occurred to me that I had never even looked into that second booth. The crafter's products had been placed flat on a table with no racks, shelves, backdrops or partitions to block my view. The third crafter, on the other hand, had used both the inside and the outside walls of his display to showcase his products. The artwork I saw in the distance was actually on the outside of his booth. If the second crafter had used her space wisely and had built herself some walls, she would have also been building herself the opportunity for better sales.

At an outdoor show, this crafter has used the white side curtains of her booth to build walls and provide a good contrasting background for her crafts.

"Good fences make good neighbors." There is a great deal of truth to this. I can recall another show where one crafter had a flat table display while the booth next to hers contained a very high display with lots of nooks and crannies. The product could be seen from the back of the display as well as from the front. Many customers entered the first crafter's booth only to reach over her tables and examine the products in the second booth. This caused ill feelings between the neighboring crafters.

Do yourself a favor. Give your display some height by giving it some walls, whether in the form of shelving, lattice, racks, screens, crates, pegboard, *anything*! to keep customer attention focused on your booth and not on someone else's.

Flexibility

Not all craft shows will offer you a $10' \times 10'$ space in which to set up your display. The space might only be 8' wide by 10' deep, or 8' deep by 10' wide, or even 6' deep by 8' wide. At other shows, you may be given a space in a corner, either the corner of a room or a corner space at the end of a row. There is also the possibility of hall space and other long and narrow booth setups . . . and "table space" setups. So creating an inflexible show display that only fits into a $10' \times 10'$ show space could make you a very frustrated crafter. You may want to participate in a show where the booth dimensions do not coincide with the size of your display.

Some crafters use their outdoor $10' \times 10'$ tent frame as the foundation for their indoor display. I would not advise this unless the size of your tent can be adjusted to accommodate different booth shapes and sizes. If you use the canopy tents standard to the industry, this is not possible. The tent is constructed in one piece. The shape and size, when set up securely, is inflexible.

If you plan to use your tent as the frame for both your indoor and outdoor display, buy a pole tent and not a canopy tent. The size of a pole tent can be adjusted merely by changing the length of the individual poles. You can always substitute longer or shorter poles to accommodate almost any booth size. The fixtures used to connect the poles would be the same no matter what length poles you use.

A flexible display is a valuable commodity. Try to find more than one use for each piece of equipment. This will give you even more creative options when setting up your display.

I sell Christmas dolls and Christmas tree skirts. My shelving units can adapt to accommodate either product alone or a combination of both products together. If I go to a show where I am only selling dolls, I have shelves to put them on. If I am selling just tree skirts, I can turn the shelving unit into a two-tier (even double-sided!) tree skirt rack. And if I want to sell both, the top half can be fitted with shelves, while the bottom half of the same piece can be used as a rack. The more flexible your display and its components, the more design possibilities you will have.

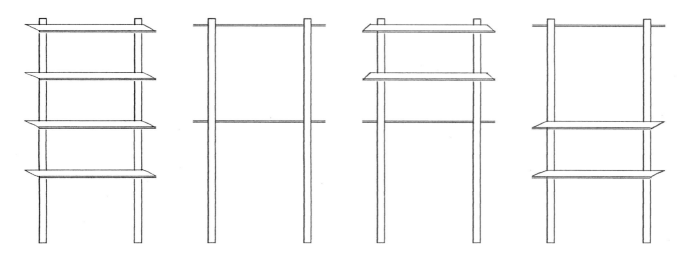

Try to find several different uses for each piece of display equipment. The more flexibility each has, the greater your display options. Shown here is one piece of my display equipment. It can be fitted with dowels (for my tree skirts), with shelving (for my Christmas dolls) or with a combination of shelves and dowels to accommodate both products at one time. This affords me myriad ways for setting up my display depending on how much of each product I have in stock or plan to sell.

A Portable Display

Make your display as portable and compact as possible. It must be able to fit in your car without seriously impacting space reserved for your product. It must also fit into a closet or other area of your home (wherever you plan to keep it) when you are not using it. Large display components—tables, shelving units and racks—should be collapsible for easy storage and as lightweight as possible for easy transporting. Don't make them so awkward that you dread the thought of moving them from one place to another. Don't use equipment so heavy that you are perspiring, exhausted and grumpy before the show even begins. There'll be no place to take a shower and you won't be in the right fame of mind for selling.

Sturdy and Stable

Customers will be forever brushing against your tables as they view your product. They will nudge your shelving units, lean on clothing racks and push against display cases. Make sure your equipment can stand up to this kind of abuse. If a customer accidentally nudges a display piece, will it wobble precariously and possibly cause your products to fall and break?

This metal art display not only offers flexibility in design, but it can also be broken down for easy transporting, taking up a minimum of storage space in your car and in your home. Photos courtesy of Elaine Martin Inc., P.O. Box 261, Highwood, IL.

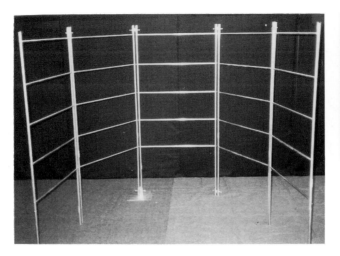

Protect your products by exhibiting them on sturdy display equipment. You want to spend your time selling your product, not picking it up off the floor.

One way to add stability to your display is to connect the large adjacent display components together with rope, wire or bungee cords. Free-standing display pieces should be securely weighted at the base with ground stakes, sandbags or other heavy materials.

Sufficient Inventory

I have attended many crafts shows as a customer, as a crafter and also as a show promoter. And because I am both a crafter and a salesman, I always watch the customers. If a crafter has a sparse display with only a few products for sale, customers just breeze by that crafter's booth. They can view in an instant all that is for sale. They walk in, walk through and walk out. There is no *reason* for them to linger. The faster customers move through your booth, the less chance you have to make a sale.

But if a substantial amount of product is presented the customer must draw closer and pause long enough to see it all. While they are looking, you can make contact and conversation with them. Immediately the chances improve for you to make a sale.

Stock your display well. You can only make money on what you bring to the show. If you display twenty pieces of product at $20 each, the most you can hope to bring home from the show is $400. And that is only if

This crafter has a good foundation for a nice display. More product is definitely needed as well as a few more pieces of interesting hardware. Right now, she is using only two planes to showcase her products. A set of shelves on either side of the lattice would make her display more interesting and give her space to display more product.

you sold absolutely everything you brought, which is highly unlikely. More likely you will sell from 10 percent to 50 percent of your inventory (two to ten pieces out of twenty) netting you between $40 to $200. Making that kind of money probably won't even cover your expenses.

But if you brought one hundred pieces of merchandise to the show, you would have the chance to sell *more* product and make *more* money. Sales of 10 percent to 50 percent of one hundred pieces of product, at $20 each, would return $200 to $1,000, a much better return on your show fee investment. And, because you have more of a selection for your customers, the percentage of sales would probably also increase.

Making product takes time and money, but participating in a crafts show takes time and money too. There's no sense wasting either unless you are prepared to reap the full reward. And to do that, you need a good amount of product to sell.

A crafter friend recently started selling at crafts shows. She has a very limited inventory but has designed a nice display for her products. When

This crafter came to sell. She carried approximately one thousand pieces of inventory. She is sure to have great sales because she is offering her customers an interesting display and a large variety of product from which to choose.

I tell her she needs to add more product, she complains it will cost money and she hasn't made any money yet. This may be true, but I wish she had observed her customers as I did at her last show. It took each of them less than a minute to see all she had to offer. They barely paused as they walked through her booth.

If you've done thorough market research, you should have enough confidence in your products and craft to invest some money into building your inventory. Don't go overboard, but do have plenty of product to fill your show space—to make it worthwhile for your customers to stop and look.

Personality and Ambience

There are many technical aspects to consider when creating a display that suits your products, but no less important is the *aesthetic* value of your display.

Give it a little personality. Create some ambience. Shop for some of your display equipment at flea markets and garage sales. You will be surprised at what you will find, reasonably priced, that will work wonders and add character to your display.

What a charming idea! The umbrella is a great touch that really adds personality to this crafter's display. Try to use equipment that adds personality and ambience to your display—something artsy! Something charming!

Take into account what you are selling. If it's antique or heirloom-flavored crafts, then flea market accessories might be just what you need to charm your customers into a purchase. If you are selling crafts with a contemporary flavor, then glitz it up a bit.

You probably think after reading this that it's a big undertaking to create an effective display for your crafts products. Well, it is and it isn't. Creating the "perfect" show booth display doesn't happen overnight. It takes some time, some planning and a little marketing savvy. It may take a year to get it all together just the way you like it, partly because the display equipment you need (or want) costs more than you can afford

There's personality written all over this freestanding display from the choice of a company name, to the rustic display (only a real tree could have been better), to the whimsical nature of the products themselves.

right now and partly because it is a matter of trial and error. You might not yet know exactly what will work and what won't work for your particular products. But your display is an investment. And, as long as you don't go overboard with high-priced equipment, you should receive a handsome return on that investment. The improvements you make will more than pay for themselves.

EVALUATING YOUR CURRENT DISPLAY

The next time you participate in a crafts show, ask yourself these questions:

Did I have trouble loading my car for this show?   ☐ Yes   ☐ No
Why? _____

Did I have trouble carrying my display to the show?   ☐ Yes   ☐ No
Why? _____

Did I have trouble setting up my display?   ☐ Yes   ☐ No
Why? _____

How long did it take me to set up?
☐ ½ hour   ☐ 1 hour   ☐ 1½ hours   ☐ 2 hours   ☐ too long

After you set up your display ask yourself the following questions:

Does my display stand out in the crowd?	☐ Yes	☐ No
Is it angled toward oncoming customer traffic?	☐ Yes	☐ No
Are all of my products visible?	☐ Yes	☐ No
Does it suit the products I am selling?	☐ Yes	☐ No
Does it showcase my products and my craft?	☐ Yes	☐ No
Does it have personality?	☐ Yes	☐ No
Can customers touch my products without my help?	☐ Yes	☐ No
Does my booth design say "Welcome!"?	☐ Yes	☐ No
Is the entrance to my booth large enough?	☐ Yes	☐ No
Is there space inside for customers to walk around?	☐ Yes	☐ No
Is there a designated "sales area"?	☐ Yes	☐ No
Does my sales area contain what I need to close a sale?	☐ Yes	☐ No
Do I have enough inventory to fill my show space?	☐ Yes	☐ No
Do I have enough inventory to interest my customers?	☐ Yes	☐ No
Are my display and its components flexible?	☐ Yes	☐ No
Is my display multi-level?	☐ Yes	☐ No
Is my display high enough?	☐ Yes	☐ No
Can I see other crafters' products from my show booth?	☐ Yes	☐ No
Can my display be changed to satisfy different booth dimensions?	☐ Yes	☐ No
Are my display and its components sturdy and stable?	☐ Yes	☐ No

Crafts Show Display Equipment
The "Hardware"

When I analyze the composition and resulting effect of any crafts show display, I tend to group the individual components into two distinct categories—the "hardware" and the "software."

The "hardware" consists of large primary equipment such as tables, shelving units, pegboard, gridwalls, lattice, screens, backdrops and racks. It also includes smaller tabletop display equipment used to showcase your products. "Hardware" includes all necessary and functional equipment.

The "software," on the other hand, refers to the more subtle embellishments that add flavor to your display—table coverings, the use of color, visual aids, signage, audio accents and lighting. These decorative accents bring your display to life.

Creating an effective crafts show display involves putting together the right combination of these two components and creating balance and harmony between them. It's somewhat like furnishing a weekend retreat. Your show booth is your home away from home. Many of your weekends will be spent there.

The Hardware

No matter what you are selling, you will no doubt need some large and small pieces of functional display equipment. Where will you find them?

What will they be made of? How will you put it all together to create a layout conducive to selling (and buying) your products?

Where to Find Display Equipment
- listed under "Display Fixtures" or under your craft or product category in the yellow pages or 800-number phone directory
- professional crafts trade publications
- general merchandise stores
- hardware stores
- home improvement and remodeling superstores
- flea markets
- garage sales
- recycling centers
- your own home
- the attics and garages of friends, family and neighbors

As I scoured flea markets and garage sales for reasonably priced display hardware, I also came across some innovative display uses for some very ordinary household items. I thought this egg carton display was especially creative. If the back end of each carton were angled up more toward the customer and if the cartons themselves were painted or covered with fabric, this would make a very nice display option for miniatures, jewelry and other small hand-crafted products.

Where to Find Hardware

Not all display hardware has to be purchased new. This is the most expensive way to build your display. You may be able to make your own display pieces. You might even have some serviceable pieces right in your own home. Use your imagination. This is where you get to employ your creativity to its fullest. It's *fun*!

PROFESSIONAL CRAFTS SOURCES

"How-to" crafts magazines are not generally a good source for craft show display equipment since they cater more to amateur home crafters who don't usually sell their products. But professional crafts publications such as show listing and trade magazines do carry ads for crafts show display merchants. Even if you don't buy any of their products, they are a valuable source of ideas. These publications also carry classified ads from crafters selling used equipment. You might find someone selling a complete display that would be perfect for your products at a very reasonable price! One excellent source for crafter hardware is Elaine Martin Inc., P.O. Box 261, Highwood, IL 60040, (847) 945-9445.

THE PHONE BOOK

You can also find display equipment listed under "Display Fixtures" in your local yellow pages or in the national AT&T 800-number telephone directory. "Display Fixtures" contains information on manufacturers and suppliers of professional trade and craft show display equipment as well as commercial displays for retail stores. Professional and commercial display equipment, for the most part, is costly, but these manufacturers also carry some reasonably priced products you can use.

Craft-specific display equipment can be found in the same directories under the heading for your particular craft (such as "Jewelry Cases") along with craft raw material suppliers, and packaging and shipping materials.

RETAIL STORES

Stroll through a few retail stores to see what they use to display products similar to yours. Though you probably wouldn't want to use the same display equipment, looking at their displays will give you some design ideas to adapt to your own display.

General merchandise stores (Bradlees, Caldor, Kmart, Wal-Mart, etc.) sell a host of household items and closet-organizer pieces adaptable for display use. Full-size and tabletop collapsible plastic shelving

Commercial gridwalls are available from most display fixture companies. With the right gridwall extensions, you can effectively display almost any product.

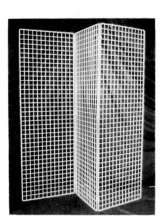

Use these extensions to suspend shelving, perpendicular to the gridwall or to hang product.

Dowels or metal rods can be threaded through this gridwall extension, making it ideal for hanging clothing (with or without hangers).

. . . to display hats.

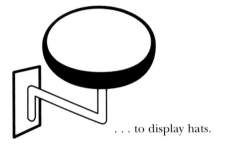

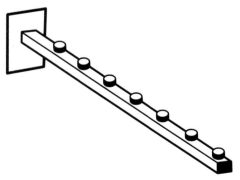

. . . for any product that has a strap or hangs, such as handbags. These can also be used to suspend hangers for clothing.

Gridwall basket extensions like those shown at right are available in a variety of sizes. They make an effective artwork display that can accommodate more than one piece of product per basket. This crafter's gridwall display of beaded scarves (at far right) is quite effective. It gives customers access to all products so they can easily browse and make a selection.

units, clothing racks, aluminum folding tables, card and snack tray tables and cardboard pedestal tables are just a few of the items you can find. These are great inexpensive alternatives to more costly professional equipment.

Home improvement and remodeling superstores as well as the larger hardware stores are also excellent sources for viable display options. They

Pegboard, sold by most commercial display fixture companies, hardware and home-building supply stores, is another option for a display background and foundation. Pegboard extensions similar to those used for gridwalls are also available to accommodate a wide variety of product.

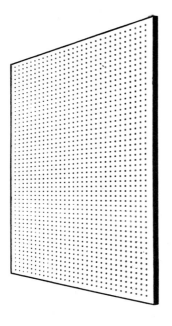

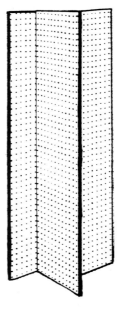

carry lattice, pegboard, wood for framing your display, wood boards for shelving, dowels for hanging your products, ladders, plywood and many, many other items that might work well for you. Use your imagination when you browse through these stores.

ONE MAN'S JUNK . . .

Flea markets and garage sales offer you the best opportunity to pick up some very conventional (and unconventional) display pieces at reasonable (even cheap) prices. Many articles left at local recycling centers can also be turned into wonderful and charming display hardware.

Before you pay full price for any display equipment, scout local flea markets, garage sales and recycling centers. You will be truly amazed at what you will find—and what people sell for practically nothing or are willing to give away!

New crafters are often poor crafters. I was no exception. Some of my original display pieces were found in my own home, tucked away in a closet. Others I usurped from the garages and attics of neighbors, friends and relatives. Don't overlook the obvious. Scour your attic (and anybody else's who'll let you) for items you can use to showcase your products and save yourself some money.

Commercial gridwall is also available in small modular panels, which can be connected to create a variety of different booth configurations such as this shelving unit. Gridwall panel displays break down easily, making them convenient to transport and store.

Flea markets are an excellent source for reasonably priced display equipment. At one flea market, in one day, I found all the pieces in the following photos, plus wooden tabletop racks, quilter's racks ($25-75) and much more. These velour jewelry display pieces ranged in price from $1 to $3. Use as is or re-cover with fabric to match your display.

Wood and Other Display Mediums

Consider wood if you are planning to make your own display hardware, especially for the larger pieces. It is versatile and can adapt well to any

These Styrofoam head mannequins ($1 each) can be covered with fabric or colored with Styrofoam paint. Use these to display hats, jewelry, scarves, etc.

This full-size mannequin ($75) is guaranteed to be a real showstopper when you dress her in your handcrafted clothing, coats, jackets, shawls, apparel and accessories.

Wooden louvre shutters ($5) make a fine display for jewelry. Taller versions are also available and can be hung or attached to your tent frame, or angled in a "V" shape for a freestanding display.

number of functional and creative designs. Wood is durable. A well-made wooden display can last for decades. Wood is also sturdy and can carry a great deal of product weight. Two-by-fours, wooden boards, dowels, molding and plywood are easily available, reasonably priced and can be fashioned into thousands of different display pieces.

Easels ($1 to $3) are versatile yet inexpensive tabletop hardware. Use them to display plates, flat wall clocks, wooden puzzles, etc., in an upright position.

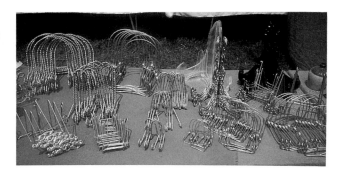

Wood is a great choice for creating custom hardware. This simple wood display—consisting of only five wooden studs—very effectively displays decorative wind chimes. The crafter might have gone one step further and provided a backdrop for his display so the product would not get confused with things in the background.

And unlike glass or metal display equipment, wood can be stained and/or painted, which allows for more decorative options. Depending on how you finish and color the wood, it can blend in or provide contrast. And if you happen to change your product line, there's a good chance you can readapt your wood pieces to fit your new product line.

Though wood is a heavy choice for display equipment, metal grids and particleboard pegboards are even heavier and more expensive. If you can find a retail store going out of business, you may be able to get metal grids and particleboard pegboards at a reasonable price. But buying them new might be cost prohibitive.

Unless you are selling contemporary crafts, chrome, glass and/or metal display pieces make for a very sterile and commercial selling environment and can detract from the personality and ambience you are trying

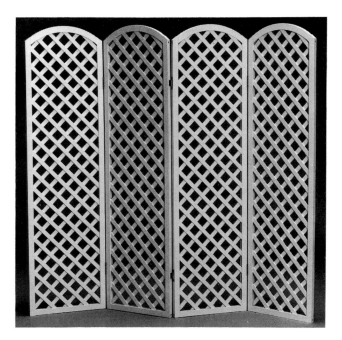

Lattice has always been a favorite hardware choice of floral crafters. It can be purchased in individual unframed wood or plastic panels from hardware, lumber or do-it-yourself home remodeling stores. It is also available fully framed and hinged as seen here from B&C Mortensen Wood Products, Rt. 4, Box 1000, Oldtown, ID 83822, (208) 437-5665. Just add product, and you are ready to sell!

Solid wood is a heavy display choice. Often crafters opt to only *frame* their display in wood and use other lighter mediums to fill the interior such as household screen or chicken wire. Thin plywood, pegboard and lattice could also have been used. A shorter version would make a versatile tabletop display.

so hard to create. But if you fill them with enough product, your customers might hardly notice they are there.

Some plastic display options have also surfaced on the market. Plastic lattice is readily available at most home centers. This may work fine if your product is lightweight, and plastic is much lighter than wood.

Modular plastic shelves are another option often seen at crafts shows. You can purchase these at most general merchandise stores (Bradlees, Caldor, Wal-Mart, Kmart, etc.) They are lightweight and convenient and may be fine for an indoor display of lightweight products. In an outdoor environment, or when displaying heavy products, however, they may not be stable enough.

Personally, I prefer wood for a crafts show display. Not only is it functional, it also creates a nice atmosphere in which to showcase your handmade products.

Wooden ladder-type displays are wonderful and versatile hardware options. Used free-standing or hinged together, they offer many different options. They can be fitted with shelves, dowels or extensions similar to those used for pegboard and gridwall displays. If you make your own and plan to use extensions, make sure the diameter of your dowels is correct for the size extensions you buy.

Rows of shelving can also be laid across two ordinary wooden ladders to create a simple display. Paint or stain the wood, or let it age naturally.

A "tree" made of wood dowels fit through a rod that's set into a wood base, is easy to make and a great choice for Christmas ornaments, hair accessories, jewelry and other products that hang. Make it short for table-top displaying or taller, using a thick closet-rod-sized dowel, for a great free-standing display. The dowels and stand should be removable for easier packing and transporting.

Using Display Tables

There are several different kinds of tables you can use in creating your display. Though I don't advocate the use of table displays as a rule, there are some crafts for which tables are the best and most convenient display choice, such as jewelry. Your show tables are a blank canvas on which you will paint an interesting picture with your products.

STANDARD TABLES

Aluminum folding tables are the standard used by most crafters. They are lightweight, easy to transport, fold in half and lay flat for storage, and

Four freestanding ladders are the foundation for the two outer hardware pieces of my own craft show display. I use them with dowels (for my tree skirts), with shelving (for my dolls) or with a combination of shelving and dowels (to accommodate both products at the same time). Because the ladders have depth, I can even turn them sideways and place *two* rows of dowels on each rung of the ladder, making a freestanding, *double-sided* display for the center of my booth.

This ladder-type display, using wood slats instead of dowels for the ladder rungs, works wonderfully well for breakables that need special protection. The walls allow some air to flow through, which lessens the ''kite'' effect that flat board construction would create, while still providing ample support for fragile products. For breakables, the shelving should always be fitted with a lip across the front to further stabilize product.

come equipped with a handle that makes them easy to carry. These tables cost between $30 and $60 at any general merchandise store.

The sizes most commonly used are $6' \times 3'$ and $7' \times 3\frac{1}{2}'$. I would suggest buying the smaller table. It will allow for more variation in how and where you place your tables and how many you can use within your show booth. Using smaller tables will also leave more room in your booth for your customers to walk about.

If your products are especially heavy, the middle section of the table, where the fold is located, should be reinforced to keep it from sagging.

Sagging often happens anyway over a period of time. Reinforce this section *before* it begins to sag or the hinges will become permanently weakened.

COMMERCIAL TABLES

Heavy commercial tables cannot be folded in half. Twice as much length will be required to store them. They don't come equipped with carrying handles, and the added weight and length will make them awkward to carry. They are also more expensive than aluminum tables.

Heavy commercial tables are, however, sturdier than aluminum tables and don't require any reinforcements because they have no weak center seam. The weight and design of a commercial table also make it more stable. If you sell very heavy or fragile products, you might have to bear the inconvenience of a heavier table in order to protect your products.

MAKING YOUR OWN TABLES

Some crafters make their own tables using plywood sheets on wooden sawhorses or aluminum legs. Covered nicely, you can hardly tell the difference. But these are the least stable of all table displays. There is nothing anchoring the plywood tabletop to the table legs. Customers nudging the table and leaning over it to look at products can shift the top right off your table.

Wooden sawhorses have been replaced by these much lighter, more compact aluminum table supports. Available from Elaine Martin Co., 444 Lake Cook Road, #1, Deerfield, IL 60015. Phone 1-800-642-1043 for more information and a crafts show display catalog.

However, a plus side to making your own tables is they can be any shape or size you want to make them. You could make a ''C'' (or any other) shape table, fitting yourself nicely into the inner part of the curve, while the outer part would push products closer to the customer (or vice versa). Homemade tables, in unusual shapes, can make your display more interesting.

CARD TABLES

Smaller, square card tables can be of tremendous value in your show booth. They fold up nicely for packing and storage and they are sturdy if you invest in a good one. They can serve as your sales table, where you write your sales slips and package customer purchases. Card tables can extend your booth area if, at the last minute, you are given more space at a show than expected.

At an outdoor show, they can often be placed outside your tent, leaving the entire inside of your tent for product display. A card table could also be used as your work station if you demonstrate your craft.

SNACK TRAY TABLES

Tray or snack tables also have their value. They are small, compact, inexpensive and can be used in place of a card table when less space is available. Snack tray tables are not very stable. I would not use them to display product, but one or two might serve well as your sales or work area.

Chairs

Plan to have a place to sit when you get the opportunity. Some crafters use webbed beach chairs; others bring metal folding chairs. It doesn't matter as long as the chair is easy to fold, store and carry.

The most commonly used by crafters are director's chairs with wood frames and fabric backs and seats. These are very comfortable and are available in two heights: regular chair height for sitting at a table, and a taller version for setup behind a high crafts display. Both can be folded for storage. New director's chairs cost between $50 and $125, but you can find used ones for about $10 to $25 at flea markets and garage sales. I purchased mine (brand new) at a Sears surplus store and paid $5 for the table-height chair and $12 for the tall chair. What a bargain!

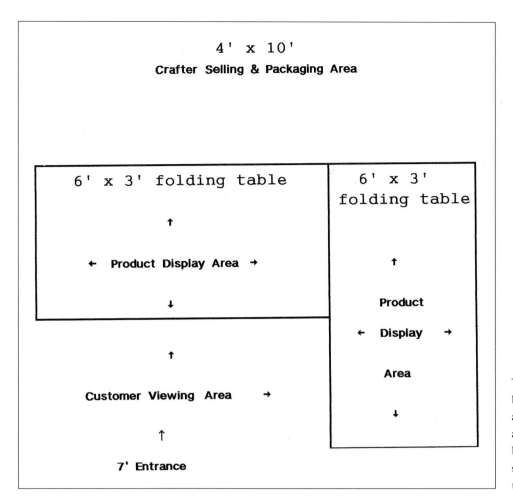

4' x 10'

Crafter Selling & Packaging Area

6' x 3' folding table

↑

← **Product Display Area** →

↓

6' x 3' folding table

↑

Product

← **Display** →

Area

↓

↑

Customer Viewing Area →

↑

7' Entrance

Table displays don't have to be boring displays. Here and on the following pages are several choices that can be used to maximize your selling space when using tables.

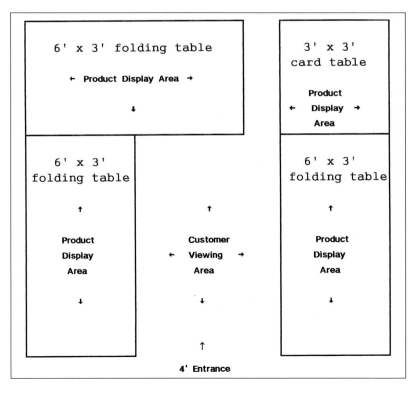

6' x 3' folding table

← **Product Display Area** →

↓

3' x 3' card table

Product
← **Display** →
Area

6' x 3' folding table

↑

Product
Display
Area

↓

6' x 3' folding table

↑

Customer
← **Viewing** →
Area

↓

↑

6' x 3' folding table

↑

Product
Display
Area

↓

4' Entrance

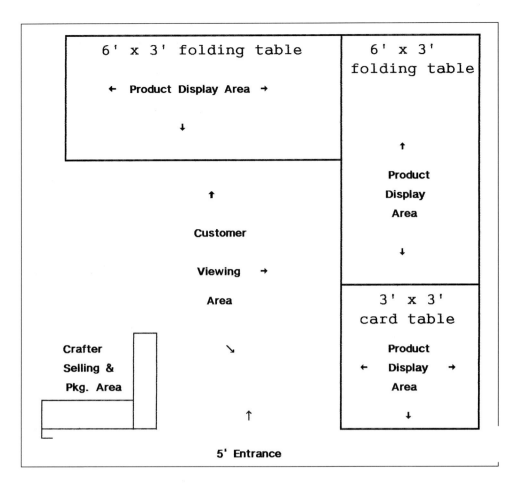

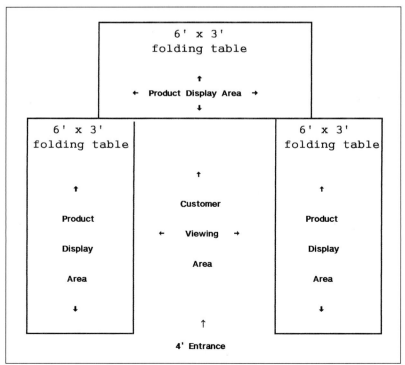

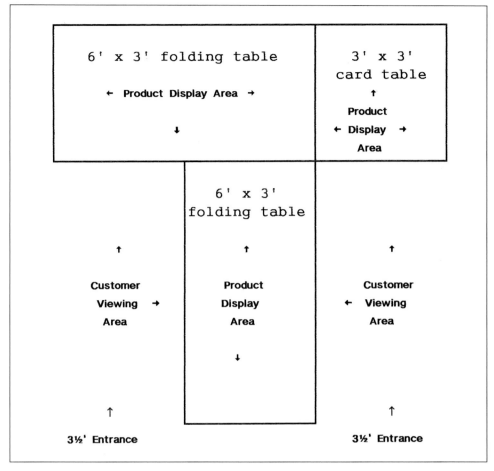

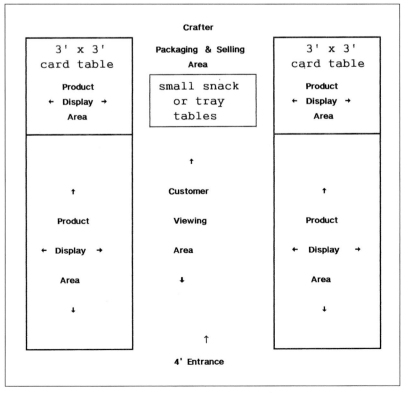

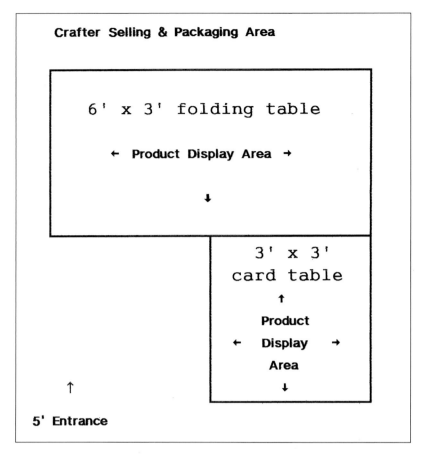

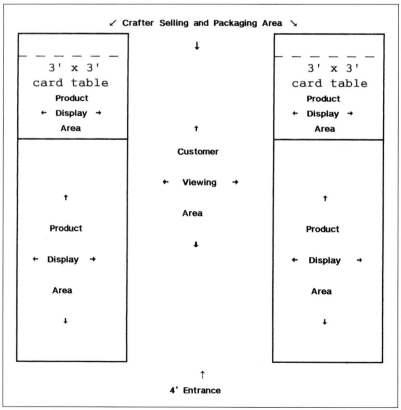

Using Your Hardware to Arrange Your Products

It is not your customer's job to make sense of your display—it's yours. Though you want to make it as interesting and varied as possible, your display should still have an underlying sense of order—a flow and connectedness that can be easily recognized. How you place and arrange your products, and how you use your hardware to segregate some products and link others, can send suggestive yet powerful buying messages to your customers.

What do you want to tell you customers about the products in your display? That one product is especially important? That another comes in a variety of different designs, colors, patterns, textures or sizes? That this

Copy, cut out and use the grids shown here and on pages 96 and 97 to position your display arrangement. Scale: each box equals one square foot.

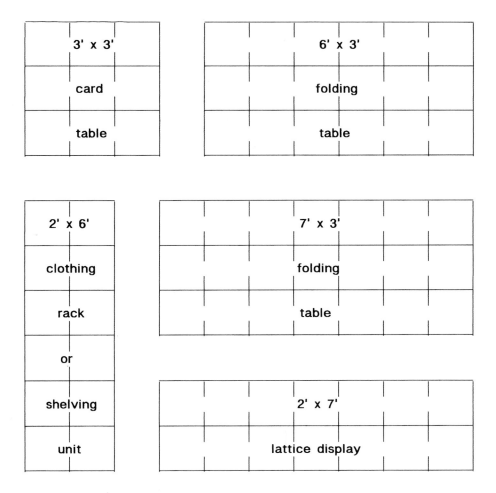

3' x 3'

card

table

6' x 3'

folding

table

2' x 6'

clothing

rack

or

shelving

unit

7' x 3'

folding

table

2' x 7'

lattice display

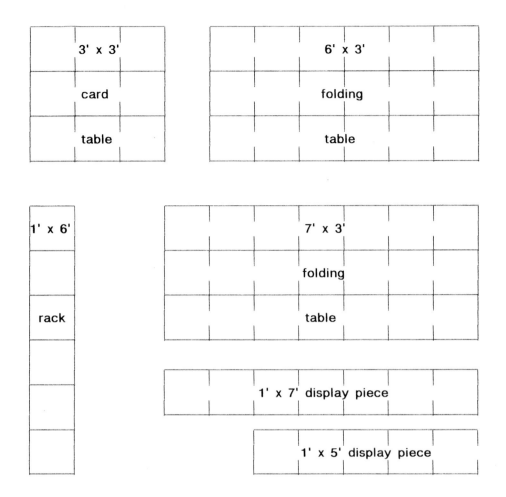

product was made to be worn or used with that product? That this scarf would look especially great with a turtleneck? That this piece of ceramic can be used as a flower vase, a fruit-filled centerpiece or a catchall on a bedroom nightstand? That this clock can be hung on a wall or set free-standing on a table? That these small paintings would make a lovely presentation clustered around this large one? That these quilts (placemats) can be mixed and matched with these pillow shams (dinner napkins) for a more eclectic look? That this leather belt is *different* from that one? That these rugs come in three different sizes?

All of these messages can be expressed through correct and creative placement of your display hardware and the products they showcase—without ever saying a word—either by isolating a product or by grouping products together.

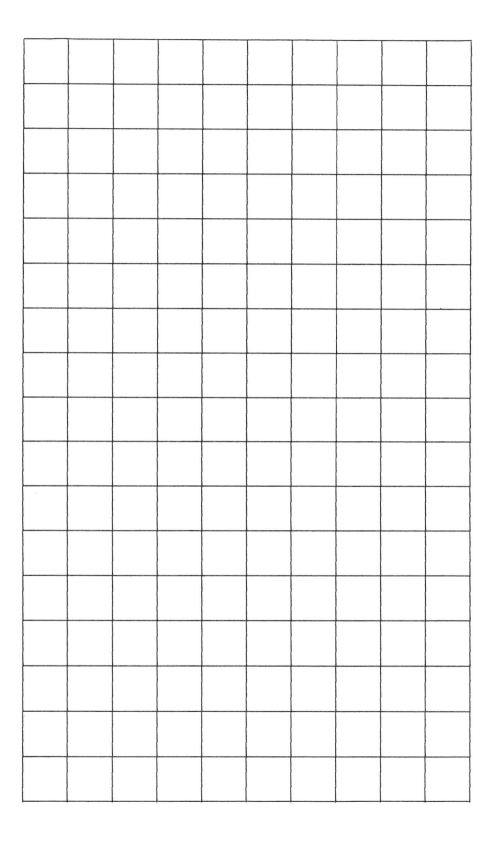

Director's chairs, the favorite choice of crafters, are available in two heights—one for sitting behind a table; the other for a more lofty vantage point.

By grouping *identical* products together, you make it easier for your customers to notice them. One of these dolls, scattered among a large array of other products, might be overlooked. Here, grouped together in a charming milk pail, they are hard to miss.

Baskets are one simple and inexpensive way to contain and group small *similar* products together within your display. This particular arrangement says, "These products are all the same—yet different. There are a variety of different fabrics and patterns for you to choose from."

Featuring a Special Product

To convey the message that one product is especially important . . . more expensive . . . of better quality . . . has more features . . . than other products in your display, give it a place of importance. Make it the focal point. Display it more prominently than the other products. Set it slightly apart, slightly higher, in the center of your display, in a

This wood crafter has used his skills not only to create an appealing product, but also to isolate this part of his product line on separate display hardware fashioned to really showcase the product. Cleverly designed, this display is hinged, both sides fold together, with a convenient clasp to hold the two sides together. A carry handle is another great feature of this mini-showcase.

Where and how you place each product conveys an underlying message to your customers. In my own display, I feature one product, on the top rung of my display, all by itself, to make it stand out. Simply by product placements, I am telling my customers, "This piece is extra special! It may be more expensive, but it's worth it!"

setting of its own. If *you* so obviously prize this piece, there's a good chance your customers will also.

Grouping Your Products

A group of products, displayed together, is always more visible than one isolated product (unless that one product is showcased). Grouping products is a great way to emphasize the similarities between products while clearly pointing out their differences.

If one of your products is available in a variety of colors, place a grouping of the product—in all colors—somewhere in your display. If you sell a selection of jewelry bracelets in different patterns, lengths and widths, show them on one piece of hardware in a group so customers can see the *differences* among them. If the same woven basket is available in small, medium and large, by all means display the three sizes together so your customers know they are connected. Even if you carry several pieces of product exactly the

This crafter is calling special attention to her dream-catcher earrings by placing them in their own display case, while the rest of her product is laid on the table.

same, group three or more of them together. It will be easier for your customer to spot a group than one product standing alone.

Clearly grouping products also offers you the chance to more than double your sales. In the case of the products with similar characteristics, sales often increase when a customer purchases more than one piece in that group to have a matching set. Though they only planned to buy the salt and pepper shaker, when they see the matching napkin holder, they won't be able to resist!

Likewise, subtle differences in the same product, when made obvious to the customer, can also lead to increased sales. When I shop for Christmas presents for my nieces, I like to buy each of them the same present, yet somehow different. I might buy them silver bracelets, each in a different design; or the same sweater, but in different colors.

Grouping products together is a valuable marketing tool. It helps customers *see* your products better, see more *value* in your products and *buy* your products. Use your large and small pieces of display hardware to set some products apart and to bring others together.

The Do's and Don'ts of Displaying

Each type of product or craft has its own unique requirements to allow for optimum use of space and to give your products as much visibility as possible.

Freestanding displays are a great way to isolate and group products. This freestanding display points out the similarity of all the products it contains, while clearly showing their differences. If the customer likes the design of these scarves, she might select several—in different colors—multiplying this crafter's chances to increase her sales.

Jewelry

Jewelry displays are busy displays. It takes a large number of individual jewelry pieces to adequately fill two or three tables. Each small piece is competing for your customer's attention.

Displaying jewelry allows for great combinations and configurations of a variety of individual showcase materials. Two or three tables, nicely covered, with the addition of the right *upright* tabletop hardware, will make a great showcase for your jewelry. Tabletop hardware is especially important when displaying small products.

Jewelry is also the craft product most vulnerable to theft. It is small yet valuable for its size. The more pieces of product you display, the more difficult it will be to keep track of them.

"A place for every product, and every product in its place." This is how some jewelry crafters keep track of their inventory. Each product has its own designated location on the table. When a space becomes vacant due to a sale, it is immediately filled with a similar product. If the ring display has an empty section, and the customer standing in front of it is

GROUPING YOUR PRODUCTS

List products you could group together.

#1 Grouped by _____ (color, subject, design, etc.)

_____   _____

_____   _____

_____   _____

#2 Grouped by _____

_____   _____

_____   _____

_____   _____

#3 Grouped by _____

_____   _____

_____   _____

_____   _____

#4 Grouped by _____

_____   _____

_____   _____

_____   _____

Tabletop hardware is especially important when selling jewelry and miniatures, where many small items are vying for your customer's attention. This is a small part of my friend Chris Gould's jewelry display. The wooden jewelry case (made by her father) not only showcases her products, but also doubles as a carrying case—complete with latch and carrying handle! The ceramic hand, painted black, was purchased at a local flea market—$7 each or 3 for $15—a very good price for a piece of display hardware that effectively groups this ring, necklace and bracelet set. For a less expensive alternative, an opera-length glove could be used—stuffed with polyfill and weighted with a brick inside.

not trying on a ring, then where is the ring? The quicker a missing product can be detected, the better the chance of recovery.

I would not advise putting all of your jewelry under glass in an effort to avoid theft. Of course, if you are selling 14k or using expensive precious stones, there may be no other way to protect them or to keep track of them. But shielding your products from theft might also shield you from sales. Jewelry, especially, is an item your customers like to touch and try on before purchasing.

Florals

Displaying floral products comes with its own set of problems. Most florals are large so it is especially important to raise your display to its full height to accommodate as much product as possible and still be able to showcase them individually. Leave some space between each displayed product so they won't rub each other and become damaged.

Florals are fragile and can't be packed too tightly when transporting them. When designing your show booth, don't choose bulky display equipment that will take up car space important to the safety of your products. Opt for flat display pieces, such as lattice, which won't take up as much car space.

Lattice is an excellent display medium for hanging florals. This crafter has used her lattice to effectively build herself some walls and enclose her show booth.

Ceramics, Pottery and Other Fragiles and Breakables

Ceramics, pottery and other fragiles and breakables can be displayed equally well on tables as on shelving units. Stable display equipment is the most important consideration when exhibiting breakables.

Secure plates on plate stands or easels. If you use shelves, include a slight lip, ledge or groove on your shelves to brace your pieces. The back of your shelves should be at least partially closed to block the wind. The display frame itself should be well anchored.

Wood Products

If you make wood crafts, I have every confidence you can create effective and efficient display hardware for your products.

Tall wood products, such as furniture, often require no additional hardware other than the products themselves. If you sell armoirs, cupboards and the like, you already have products that would make natural walls around your display area. Displaying them along the perimeter of your show booth will leave the center part of your show space for other products.

If you sell shorter, smaller pieces such as stools, chairs and coffee tables, you still have some air space to work with. Build your display *up*. Do stack some of your pieces, but protect stacked pieces from one another to prevent damage. Don't stack them so high you can't comfortably get to the one on the bottom should a customer show interest in it.

If you have decorative tops on your wood pieces, *don't* stack them because your customers won't be able to see your artwork.

Build walls to display your wood shelves—to show how they will look on your customer's own walls.

Set smaller products, such as bowls and plates, on an upright angle so customers will get a full view of the product and not just a side view.

Apparel and Accessories

I think clothing crafters are the biggest offenders when it comes to taking the easy way out and displaying products on tables. Tables might be okay if you use enough upright hardware to make your products visible, but by themselves, they are not the right vehicle for displaying clothing.

Clothing should be *hung*—on hangers, on clothing racks or on mannequins—so your customers can see it all and visualize how the product will look on them. Clothing is large enough to be seen from a distance. Make use of its size to grab your customer's attention.

Your products are large enough to be seen from a distance. Make proper use of their size to grab your customers' attention. Display apparel and accessories as they are meant to be worn. Don't make the mistake of thinking your customers can *imagine* how your products will look on them. Show them!

Use mannequins and dress and shirt forms to showcase your clothing. Use styrofoam head forms for hats, scarves and other accessories. These don't have to be expensive—you could make your own mannequins and forms from wood, cardboard, papier-mâché or Styrofoam.

A full-body three-dimensional commercial mannequin (like the ones seen in retail stores) costs between $150 and $400. A commercial "torso" (from the waist up) costs about half as much. A metal, wood, cardboard

These three ladies would add a new dimension to any clothing or accessory display. Mannequins are a necessity when selling wearables. Shop at flea markets to find these invaluable treasures at reasonable prices.

Head mannequins add visual interest to your display and can be made from wicker (as this one is), Styrofoam or papier-mâché (made yourself)! If you sell scarves or hats, a head mannequin is a must!

or plastic shirt or dress form would cost even less, and it doesn't have to be three-dimensional. Just an outline would do as well.

A Styrofoam head form (for hats and scarves) costs about $2 and can be covered with fabric or painted with Styrofoam paint to match your display. Molded or wood commercial head forms cost from $5 to $50.

A wooden frame display with dowels also works well for apparel. The dowels slip through both arm slots and the shirt or dress hangs down from there.

Pegboards and metal gridwalls with commercial extensions to accommodate hangers are another more commercial option for displaying clothing.

Clothing racks can also be used. Most of them are collapsible or can be easily disassembled for transporting. They are lightweight and take up a minimum of storage space. Clothing displayed on racks gives customers easy access to them. Since racked clothing is facing the customer at a

Help your customers visualize how the clothing accessories you sell can be worn with different colors . . . with different necklines . . .

sideways angle, make sure that sample products are also displayed facing the customer.

If your clothing products must be tried on before purchasing, you should provide a dressing room. If you sell apparel or accessories, include a mirror as part of your display.

Any displayed fabric craft should be free from wrinkles. Nothing looks worse (or discourages sales) more than crumpled-looking clothing hanging from a display.

For hats, by all means use hat trees (plant stands can also be used).

Metalcrafts

If your metalcrafts are made from tin, copper or any other light or thin metal, they can be displayed nicely on either shelves or tables. If you sell larger, heavy metal pieces such as estate fencing or tall iron plant hangers, your display equipment needs to be strong enough to accommodate these. Metal plant and bird-feeder stands, and other pole-type products such as lawn ornaments, are often displayed standing up in wood blocks with holes bored in them.

Fabric

Quilt racks—made from wooden dowels in a wooden frame—are the best choice for displaying handmade quilts, blankets and a host of other fabric crafts.

Hang fabric products over sanded, sealed dowels rather than over

Hat stands offer you the opportunity to display a large quantity of product in a small space. The more product you bring to a show, the more product you have the opportunity of selling. This is a full-size free-standing hat stand. A tabletop version of the same display is also available, along with hat stands that can be attached to the vertical poles of a tent.

If you sell clothing that can't be slipped over the clothing your customers are already wearing, then it's a good idea to provide a dressing room. Most people won't buy a product until they see if it will fit (and look well) on them. This dressing room can be easily assembled and is available from Elaine Martin, Inc.

wood pieces that have edges that can splinter and create "pulls" in the fabric.

Fabric products such as kitchen and bath towels, and table linens are lightweight and can also be displayed using dowels.

Fabric products also display nicely on foldable laundry drying racks. But these racks are only about two and one-half feet high and will not provide enough of a backdrop for your display. They can be used as supplemental hardware or can be placed on a table, but you will still need taller hardware around the perimeter of your show booth to close it in.

For larger and heavier fabric products, wooden dowels are often the best choice. A very nice display can be made from vertical two-by-fours with horizontal dowels. Dowels are sold in 3-foot and 4-foot lengths, or you can have them cut in longer lengths. Make sure the dowel is thick enough to hold your product without sagging.

Foldable laundry drying racks make a nice display for table linens, light quilts, baby bibs and a host of other fabric products.

Your products can be draped over them or you can use hangers. I've also found that heavy black clamp-type paper clips, called bulldog clips, are an excellent way to hang fabric products from dowels. (You can get these at office supply stores.) The clips are gentle on the fabric, will not leave a mark and can hold some very heavy fabric pieces.

Paper Products

Paper products, without any framework or backing, are very lightweight. Display pen-and-ink notecards, invitations, origami, silhouette art, quilling or other light paper products in holders or gift boxes to keep them in place. *Don't* use bungee cords stretched across your tables—it will look more like a flea market display than a crafts display.

Paper products are also more susceptible to dust, dirt and moisture. Once they come in contact with these, your creations may become unsalable. If your paper products have been laminated or sealed with an acrylic sealer, they will be moisture resistant. If they are framed or protected by glass or lucite, then you have little to worry about. But if they are not sealed, your products must be packaged to protect them.

Plastic zipper bags might be your first packaging choice, but plastic bags promote condensation. A wet paper product is a ruined paper product.

Package your products in cellophane (which does not promote condensation) instead of plastic. Don't use the cellophane wrap from the supermarket. Buy the clear stiff cellophane available at party or card stores used to wrap gift baskets.

Shrink-wrap also works well for paper products. Just make sure the products are thoroughly dry before shrink-wrapping. And have a sample unshrink-wrapped set available for customers to look at.

Lucite literature holders are a good tabletop hardware choice for displaying flat paper products such as notecards. Tall, free-standing commercial swivel displays with lucite holders also work well. Using lucite will not detract from your products—you can see right through it! An excellent source for lucite holders and other display products is Siegel Display Products, P.O. Box 95, Minneapolis MN 55440, phone (800) 626-0322.

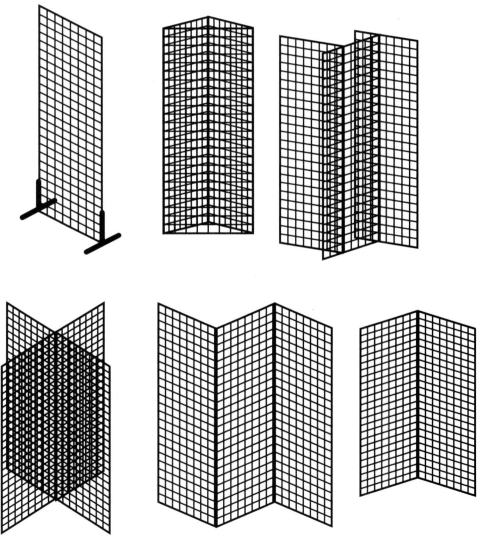

Artwork needs to be hung—as it would be in the homes of your customers—to be seen and appreciated. Metal gridwalls offer a variety of solutions and configurations for hanging art.

Artwork

If you are selling one-of-a-kind artwork, it is especially important to build your display *up* and make total use of your space. Three entire walls of your display should be covered with your creations. Add to that a free-standing center carousel of additional art in an "X," "L" or "V" shape, and flip-through portfolios at either outer corner of your display, and you are set!

Artwork should be *hung* for display as it would be hung in your customer's home so they can envision it there.

Picture frames are a personal item. If you provide frames for your artwork, the frame you choose may or may not be what your customer would choose. The right frame could clinch a sale; the wrong frame may discourage it.

Framing each piece of artwork can also be very expensive. You will have to inflate the price of the product to cover the cost of the frame. This could make a painting or drawing cost prohibitive to a customer who might otherwise have purchased it. Mats are a better choice for artwork. If you have a few spectacular pieces in your display you especially want to showcase, then frame them, but frame them conservatively both from a cost and a design perspective.

Stacked wooden crates make an effective and charming display for dolls. As a bonus, you can use the crates to pack and transport your product and to build walls in your show booth.

Dolls

Displaying your dolls on tables or shelves works well enough, but give some thought to decorative hardware that can really accent your creations. To add interest, *pose* each doll. Display some sitting, others standing, some with their legs crossed. Give them personality! To showcase and separate one doll from another, display some in chairs, on bicycles, with tissue paper nestled in a gift box . . .

If you use tables to display the dolls, raise the table up twelve to fifteen inches. Stack your product storage boxes on the table underneath your table cover, in a step pattern so each row of dolls is clearly visible.

Display Embellishments

The "Software"

Your display software should enhance your crafts presentation and bring your show booth to life. By using three of your customers' five senses—sight, sound and smell—you can subtly communicate and reinforce your message by making your display more interesting.

The Use of Color

Don't underestimate the importance of color when designing your crafts show display. The shade of your table covers, the stain on your wood hardware, and other touches of color can help sell your product. Accent your display with just the right touch of color.

Choose colors and a color scheme that won't overshadow your products. They should enhance but not compete. Don't use busy, loud or wild print fabrics; in fact, don't use any bright or patterned fabric. It may have the opposite effect of what you intended and actually draw the viewer's attention *away* from your products. Bright colors and busy, patterned fabrics may make your display more conspicuous, but they will also make your products less noticeable.

Don't choose display colors that blend in with your products either. If you are selling light or neutral-colored products, do not use a beige tablecovering or natural wood stain for your display. Use a medium-dark wood stain and deep, rich (but not bright) colored fabrics. Instead of red, try burgundy; instead of yellow, try mustard; instead of Christmas green, use hunter green. Deep rich colors are often associated with quiet but expensive good taste, an attitude very conducive to selling your crafts.

Before selecting a background color for your display, pose one of your most exemplary products in a variety of colored backgrounds to determine which best suits your product.

Depending on your product, you might want colors that contrast with your products to make your crafts stand out. In other cases, you might be better off with more subtle colors that complement rather than contrast. Experiment with both contrasting and complementary colors and see which works best for your particular products. Take color photographs of one of your most typical products (or group of products) against a variety of different backgrounds. Then imagine each on a larger scale—your whole display. For more ideas, visit a few crafts shows and see what colors other crafters use to showcase products similar in color to yours.

Don't use too many colors in your display. Limit yourself to two colors. If you are using tables, an easy way to do this is to use one shade for your table covering and skirt and use the second color for your small display hardware and/or fabric overlays.

If your display doesn't allow for any extensive use of color (if it's all wood), you can add color accents by draping fabric over shelves or by painting or staining the wood to suit your products. In addition to the typical shades of brown wood stain available, acrylic craft paint can also be used to stain wood. Apply it thinly and evenly with a slightly dampened sponge instead of a paint brush. The paint will soak into the wood instead of coating it and will allow the natural grain of the wood to show through.

A patterned background color or fabric creates confusion and more often than not makes it hard to distinguish between the product and the background. Also, choosing a color similar to that of your products makes them less visible.

Think of the variety of colors you have to choose from! Remember to seal the wood after you stain it to avoid transferring the color to your products.

If your product colors are already vibrant enough, adding additional color may only confuse your customers. In that case, stick to a basic contrast color such as black, brown, beige or white. Experiment and see which one works best for you.

Visual Aids

Small but interesting visual aids, peppered throughout your display, will give you a reason to communicate with your customers and for them to speak with you. Tools of your trade, crafts works in progress, and other "props" will encourage your customers to ask questions. The more of a rapport you build with customers, the better the chance of a sale.

Props

Many jewelry crafters display large chunks of raw uncut stone to show the origin of their products. This "before and after" approach seems to fascinate customers, and generates interest and promotes communication.

Involve your customers' senses:

Sight: The use of *color* in your display, the type and message of your *signage,* interesting marketing "*props*" displayed at your booth, how you dress for the show and other visual aids can enhance your product's appeal.

Sound: Adding soft *music* and other noninvasive *audio* accents to your presentation conveys a subliminal message to the customer about buying your products.

Smell: The scent of flowers, cinnamon, clove, and other light and pleasant yet familiar fragrances will relax your customers and put them in a buying mood. "Aromatherapy" can be a very effective sales tool.

In my own display I have two props that each garner their own kind of modest attention. The first and largest is a full-size artificial Christmas tree. It is not only a prop, it also serves an important function. Customers interested in buying my Christmas tree skirts can try them on the tree to see how they will look before they purchase them.

I added the second prop to my booth as a matter of convenience, having no idea the attention it would receive and the customer conversations it would initiate. It's a mailbox, decorated in a Christmas motif, where I keep my business cards and customer handouts. It's always open on a shelf where customers can reach in and help themselves. For some reason, they find this charming and always remark about it, which starts the conversation going in the right direction.

What props can *you* use to help sell your products? Find some that will initiate customer conversation, and you are already on your way to making a sale.

Tools of the Trade

Whatever tools you use to create your products, bring some to the show. If you plan to demonstrate your craft, you'll need them anyway, but bring some even if you don't plan to demonstrate. A jeweler's loop, casually placed on your table and occasionally used, will tell your customers, without words, that you know what you're doing.

Display an unfinished product, along with the tools you will use to finish it. A work-in-progress needlepoint, woodcarving, painting or quilt will create customer interest and verify that your products are indeed lovingly handmade.

One Special Piece

Show people what you can *really* do. I tell crafters they should have one special craft piece on display—one piece that shows the mastery and full extent of their crafting skills. The most expensive, the most interesting, the most intricate and perhaps largest piece in your booth, one piece to make your customers say, "Wow!"

At one of my earlier crafts shows I realized the importance of such a piece. Though I never expected to sell it, I was proud of the work I had done and wanted to show it off. It was a hand-quilted, hand-appliquéd Christmas tree skirt embellished with sequins and seed pearls. Little did I know at the time the value of this piece. It made people come into my booth. It made them stop and look. Some asked questions; others just made a few nice comments. All gave me a chance to speak with them without seeming to push them into a sale.

Then, at one show, a lady came to my booth and said, "I like that one." I smiled and thanked her for the compliment, which I had heard many times before. "No," she said, "I want to *buy* it," the most expensive piece in my whole booth, costing more than twice as much as any other piece. For a moment I stood there speechless (a condition that doesn't happen very often). But I quickly recovered and closed the sale.

Crafter Résumé

Ceramic and pottery crafters often display a written descriptive and pictorial essay of how their products were created. Photographs of any kind will make a customer pause. The longer they pause, the more interested they may become.

This is where your crafter résumé comes into play. Though you don't want to relegate too much of your display space to blowing your own horn, a little crowing can go a long way in gaining customer attention. Reserve a small corner of your booth area to display your résumé.

Dressing for Success

When I entered the workforce, someone told me to "dress as you wish to be perceived." It's as good a code for crafters to follow as for those in the corporate world.

You are a crafter, an *artisan*. Don't dress as if you were going to the office when you are selling your crafts. A little flamboyance, a bit of character, the *flavor* of your crafts incorporated into your attire—all will add to your customer appeal.

Dress nicely—clean and neat, sort of a "dressed-up causal" look. No T-shirts or sweatshirts, please (unless you are selling them). If you are selling products you can wear, by all means wear them at the show. That includes jewelry, hats, belts and scarves. Show your customers how your products will look on *them*.

If you are an artist, indulge yourself and look a little *artsy*! Wear a smock! If you are a wood craftsman, overalls might give the impression of a woodcrafter hard at work. If you selling Victorian craft products, add some lace, a shawl, even some velvet to your outfit! Kitchen products? How about an apron, chef's hat or both.

Some crafters go to great lengths to dress up for a show. One crafter, selling clown marionettes, dressed to look like one of her products and even acted like a clown! Customers and their children stopped to look and were drawn to buy from this crafter. She made her customers smile. I *love* to see customers smiling—it usually means better sales.

If your craft or products don't lend themselves to any particular dress code or theme, or if you feel that dressing in "costume" somehow diminishes the professional nature of your craft business, then don't do it. The idea is not to make you look foolish or feel uncomfortable. It is simply to add a touch more atmosphere and to create a memorable—and positive—visual image.

Some crafters dress more subtly, adding just a hint of flavor. This works also. The message, though more subliminal, is still conveyed.

Words may go in one ear and out the other, often forgotten soon after they are uttered. Visual images, on the other hand, linger long after the stimulus is removed.

Signage

If the show is busy, you may not be able to speak personally with every potential customer. Or a new crafter, still a bit uneasy about talking to customers, can use other methods to impart information that will leave a lasting impression. One way is by adding *signs* to your booth. Remember, signs can augment personal contact, but they are no substitute for it.

Small tidbits of information, strategically placed throughout your booth, will say what you may not have the time or opportunity to tell every customer: titles of your products, the theme of a particular group of paintings, the names of your dolls, descriptions of the stones used in your jewelry, your craft technique and process—what it is called and information about its origin and history, that you accept custom orders, where your next show will be. Signs supplement your verbal presentation.

All of my signs are enclosed in upright clear, inexpensive lucite frames. This keeps them clean and neat and I can change or replace them anytime. You can also decorate these frames with a little imagination and some glue. Why not have them done in calligraphy?

Table Dressings

The most obvious choice for decorating your tables would be to use large fabric pieces and gathered table "skirts." Some crafters use simple table-cloths when they first start selling. Others make their own table coverings. This is fine as long as you cover your tables to the floor on all sides visible to your customers. Do *not* use bed sheets; *do* make sure the edges of your fabric are nicely finished.

Overlaying more than one fabric creates a nice effect. In a Victorian-themed booth, a crochet shawl over a rich-colored table covering will add another dimension to your display. A dark-color fabric over a light one (or vice versa) creates an interesting effect.

When you think of covering your tables, don't limit your choices to fabric only. Many other mediums might better enhance your presentation. This crafter chose bamboo poles to accent her display and reinforce the theme of her product—bamboo flutes.

Velvet is often used for Victorian crafts. Suede, felt and/or velvet are popular for jewelry. Cotton and cotton blends are used to display most other products.

When you think of covering your tables, don't limit your choices to fabric only. There are other options. At one Easter show, my table display featured a "playground" filled with bunnies on bicycles, fabric eggs and other Easter products. The tables were covered with astroturf and bordered with miniature white fencing. This was a very successful display. Astroturf would also work well for golf, outdoor or sport theme products.

Explore unconventional mediums for covering or accenting your tables and other display hardware—carpeting, canvas, leather-look fabrics, etc. Add some *texture*! Take a walk through your local home improvement superstore. Browse through a fabric shop. Find something that really shows off your product and carries through on its theme. Make sure whatever you choose is washable or easy-care—dry cleaning bills can mount up quickly.

Lighting

There must be lights! You expect a show to provide adequate lighting to display your crafts. But you don't always get what you expect. Some show locations will be lighted better than others. Some will only have spotlighting instead of light distributed evenly throughout the room. If you are lucky enough to be the crafter situated directly under the source of light, your products will have an added selling advantage. If you are not, your products will be less noticeable and you may lose valuable sales because of it. The lighted booths will stand out and say, "Look at me," while those in the shadows will seem recessed and less important. Avoid being in the shadows.

Some show producers offer the option of being positioned near an electrical outlet so you can plug in your own light sources. Often, there is an additional charge for this service. Whenever electricity is offered, take advantage of it, even if it costs you money. It will probably also *make* you money.

If you provide your own light at a show, bring at least two UL-approved lamps to cross-light your booth. Do *not* use cheap aluminum lamps that cost about $10 each. These are very dangerous. The light bulb can explode and the dome cover gets extremely hot to touch. Someone may get burned. Most show promoters insist on professional lighting. These are more expensive (about $25 to $50), but they are more durable and safer than their cheaper counterparts.

Bring at least one 100-foot heavy-duty extension cord, two extra light bulbs, a UL-listed power strip/surge protector and two rolls of wide electrical or duct tape in case you have to run your extension cord across a customer aisle.

At shows where electricity is not offered, you have three choices. You can (1) use whatever light is available and hope for the best, knowing other crafters are in the same situation (which makes for an even playing field), (2) bring your lighting equipment anyway and hope you're situated near a usable electrical outlet, or (3) arm yourself with portable lighting equipment, such as the battery-powered lights used by campers.

When supplying your own light source at a show, you will need:
- UL-approved lamps/lights
- spare lamp bulbs
- 100-foot extension cord (at least one)
- UL-listed power strip
- wide electrical or duct tape

Aromatherapy

Just as the aroma of home cooking whets your appetite and makes you hungry, other smells can evoke a pleasant (and profitable) response from your customers. Aromatherapy is an effective marketing tool: cinnamon, cloves and pine for Christmas, florals in spring, citrus, vanilla and spices almost anytime. Mildly scenting your booth can help you sell.

But bear in mind that some people are especially sensitive to fragrance. Others may even be allergic to it. Use scent lightly and sparingly. Too many different or too-strong scents assaulting your customers all at once will only make them hold their noses and run for some fresh air. Try to keep it within the confines of your own show booth so it won't compete with other crafters' booths and the scent of their products.

This also includes your own perfume or cologne. Don't wear any that is different from or that might compete with the aromas in your show booth.

Your display software is just as important as your hardware. Hardware makes products more manually and visually *accessible* to your customers; software is used to make them more *noticeable.*

PUTTING IT ALL TOGETHER FOR AN EFFECTIVE CRAFTS SHOW DISPLAY

Let's take each step, one at a time, and build the ideal show booth in which to sell your crafts.

LARGE HARDWARE

Begin with the large hardware—the frame of your display.

1. Draw your large hardware pieces on a sheet of paper, leaving spaces between each piece.

    You don't have to be an artist to do this, you just have to be able to recognize one piece from the other.

    a. If you haven't yet purchased or made any hardware for your display (or if you're trying to decide on what new hardware you should buy), sit back, close your eyes and envision the display of your dreams. Now focus on the individual hardware pieces that could make up that display and draw them.

    b. If you are using folding tables as your large hardware, select and copy the table display setups from chapter 6 that you like best.

2. Photocopy each of your drawings at least ten times and cut out the hardware pieces individually.

3. Lay one set of hardware on a sheet of paper and arrange it into a $10' \times 10'$ booth configuration. Tape it to the sheet of paper.

    Start with a simple booth plan or the tone you are currently using.

4. Take a second set of hardware drawings and switch the pieces around. Try to make as many different arrangements as possible. Tape each different arrangement to a separate sheet of paper.

5. What would happen if you duplicated an existing piece of hardware? How would two of those pieces look in your display instead of one? Try it.

6. What would happen if you eliminated a piece of hardware? Try it.

7. What would you replace it with? Draw alternative hardware options.

8. Design new booth arrangements using the new hardware.

    Which ones would work? Which ones wouldn't?

9. Design booth arrangements for a space *smaller* than $10' \times 10'$. ($8'$ deep $\times 10'$ wide; $10'$ deep $\times 8'$ wide; $8' \times 8'$)

10. Design a few booth arrangements for a *larger* space.

    How can you easily expand your booth setup?

11. Design a booth plan for a $5' \times 20'$ *hallway* space.

    A one-sided display against a wall.

12. Draw your floor plan for a end-of-the-row booth.

    Hint: Two sides have customer access.

13. If your large hardware is arranged around the perimeter of your show booth, then add a freestanding or pedestal display piece in the center or corner of your booth. This would provide additional space to show more product. Draw some freestanding hardware pieces your might use and try them in your booth arrangements. How do they look?

SMALL HARDWARE

Draw display cases, boxes and any other small hardware and incorporate them into your display drawings.

SOFTWARE

Now it's time to add the finishing touches to your show booth.

Color and Texture

1. Select a two-color scheme you have tested that goes well with your products.

   a. _____

   b. _____

2. Color in your display with colored pencils.

3. What fabric and/or textures would best complement and add to the *flavor* of my products?

   a. _____

   b. _____

   c. _____

Audio Accents

What type of music could I play to give my booth more ambience:

_____

What other sounds could I use to get my customers in the mood to buy my products?

   a. _____

   b. _____

Scent Enhancements

The following scents would complement my products and soothe my customers:

   a. _____

   b. _____

Visual Aids

What visual aids would make my booth more interesting?

Props I can use to enhance my presentation:

   a. _____

   b. _____

   c. _____

   d. _____

Tools of my trade:

   a. _____

   b. _____

   c. _____

   d. _____

A work-in-progress I could bring to the show:

_____

What is the one special piece I could display?

_____

Where and how will I display it?

_____

_____

Where and how will I position my crafter résumé?

_____

How can I dress at the show to enhance the image of my crafts:

_____

_____

What signs can I use to impart information to my customers:

a. _____

b. _____

c. _____

d. _____

What messages do I want to convey to my customers?

How will I _visually_ communicate them?

Message: _____

Visual: _____

Message: _____

Visual: _____

Message: _____

Visual: _____

Audio Accents

Some crafts shows provide their exhibitors and customers with music. Others don't. I always bring a tape player and some classical, holiday or theme music to a show, just in case no one thought of it. Music is a universal language and a mood elevator. This cannot help but increase your chance of selling. The music you choose should be soft, noninvasive and upbeat.

But music is not the only sound you can use to put your customers in a good mood. Many audiotapes on the market simulate different sounds in nature. If one of them suits your product line, by all means use it when it doesn't interfere with other audio accents at the show: Indian chants for southwestern products, cowboy poetry or a Gene Autry/Roy Rogers tape when selling leather belts and buckles. You can easily create your own audiotapes.

One crafter, selling birdhouses, plays tapes of birds singing. It's really quite a nice effect. You feel like you are outside bird-watching. Are there any sounds you can think of to put customers in the mood to buy your products?

Outdoor Crafts Show Displays

Showing your crafts in an outdoor selling environment brings with it a whole new set of display challenges along with some wonderful opportunities. Let's start with the disadvantages of outdoor selling. I like to get the bad news out of the way first.

The Disadvantages of Outdoor Selling

The first piece of bad news about outdoor selling is the cost. Outdoor show equipment—tents, canopies, side curtains and other incidentals—is expensive. Crafters often don't have the cash to invest in these items while they are still trying to buy raw materials and pay for show space.

Second, there is the issue of storage space in your car. You want to bring as much product as possible to the show. How can you do this and still reserve space in your vehicle for your tent and its accessories?

And an outdoor show is never a sure thing. Inclement weather can cause a show to be cancelled, leaving you high and dry for both the show fee and the sales dollars you missed, not to mention the raw materials you purchased and the inventory you stockpiled.

Finally, selling at outdoor shows can be risky business. There's always the chance that the elements—wind, dust, rain and moisture—will damage or destroy your carefully created products and display equipment. Damaged *anything* is an expense you cannot afford.

You would think that all of these disadvantages would discourage anyone from ever selling at an outdoor show, wouldn't you? Yet many crafters actually prefer outdoor selling. Why? Here comes the good news . . .

The Advantages of Selling Outdoors

Using your tent frame in place of bulky display hardware will free more space in your car to transport product. This crafter has handily displayed her hair accessories using only the frame of the tent and some vinyl webbing. Each and every product is visible and accessible to the customer. If you can find a way to use your tent frame as the foundation for your display, setup and breakdown for a show can be easy and convenient.

At an outdoor show, your booth space will probably be larger than it would be at an indoor crafts show for two very good reasons. First, outdoor shows are usually held in a larger area such as a park, school grounds or a town green. The show parameters are not as restrictive as in a defined indoor area surrounded by four walls. Second, larger spaces are necessary to accommodate show tents and other peripherals.

At some outdoor shows, you may be able to park your car right in your show space, behind your tent. This is a wonderful convenience that allows for quick and easy setup and breakdown. And, should the weather turn ugly, your products can be moved out of harm's way in record time.

Natural light is another benefit of outdoor selling. It will make your products sparkle and will enhance their colors. You won't need to pack your own light sources—Mother Nature will provide!

Outdoor shows are highly visible shows, which can mean better customer attendance. While indoor shows depend solely on signs and advertising to bring in the customers, an outdoor show creates its own advertising just by being there. The sight of row upon row of tents filled with tons of colorful products is difficult for a passerby to resist.

And, if you are creative, your tent equipment need not usurp car space meant for product. The tent itself can actually substitute for some of the large hardware you would need for an indoor show, freeing even more space in your car to store product.

Though there are a few inconveniences associated with selling outdoors, there are also many valid reasons why outdoor selling is so popular with crafters. The trick to selling successfully at outdoor shows is to be prepared for anything and everything that might happen. This means you must arm yourself with the right equipment and use that equipment wisely and efficiently. If you do this, exhibiting at outdoor crafts shows will be fun and hassle-free.

The advantages of outdoor selling:
- Show spaces are usually larger to allow for tents and guide ropes, and some of this space can be used to display additional product.
- Outdoor shows are more visible to the public than indoor shows, which means the possibility of additional drive-by customer traffic.
- You can use your tent frame in place of some large hardware, leaving more room in your car to pack more product.
- Natural light will enhance your products' true colors and no additional light source or fixture is necessary.
- You may be able to park your car within your show space, which will make packing and unpacking significantly easier.

The disadvantages of outdoor selling:
- Wind, dust and rain can damage product and equipment.
- Bad weather may cause a show to be cancelled.
- Additional (and costly) tent equipment is required.
- Some product space in your car will be allocated for tent equipment.

Tents and Other Outdoor Equipment

Tents are *the* most important piece of outdoor show equipment. They protect you and your products from wind, rain and the unrelenting rays of a hot summer sun.

There are so many different styles of tents to choose from that it may be difficult to decide which is the right one for you. Cost, of course, will be a factor. You can't spend more than you can afford. Construction is also important. Your tent should be stable and sturdy. Ease of assembly should also be a concern. Can you set it up and take it down by yourself?

Finally, you must weigh the cost against the value of your purchase. Does one tent have added features? More flexibility? Will one last many years while another will barely survive one show season? Is one type of tent better for displaying your products than another?

A tent is a major purchase and one not to be taken lightly. Do some investigating before you invest. Go to several outdoor crafts shows. Arrive early and watch the crafters set up. Take note of which tents are used most often, how easily they are carried, how they set up and how they look. If allowed, *help* a few crafters put up their tents. Nothing teaches better than doing. This will help you decide which type of tent is best for you.

All of the tents pictured (as well as other tent options) are available from Elaine Martin, Inc. See page 80 for address and phone number.

What to look for in a tent:

- Reasonable price
- Solid and sturdy construction
- Ease of assembly
- Waterproof tops and sides
- White or neutral color canopy

Gazebos

Gazebos have grown tremendously popular over the last few years as an inexpensive alternative to the more pricey professional canopies used by most veteran crafters. You can buy them in the camping and outdoor sections of most general merchandise stores for $50 to $150. They come in sizes ranging from 9'6" to much larger. Buy the one closest in size to ten feet square. If you must, buy one slightly larger rather than slightly smaller than ten feet. One word of advice: buy them on sale in the spring.

Gazebos are not nearly as sturdy as canopy or pole tents. The support poles are lightweight and can be easily bent. Strong winds may be a problem, but the gazebo should be able to withstand anything less than that.

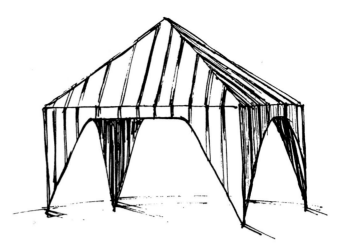

Gazebo tops are colored in bold stripe patterns, which is a problem for many crafters. When the sun shines through, the color of the tent top can alter the product color, especially jewelry. Choose the most neutral color possible. Yellow is better than green or blue; white or off-white are best.

Some gazebos come with waterproof tops; others are equipped with a mesh top that is not waterproof. If you choose one with a mesh top, purchase a plastic liner to waterproof it. Most have peaked roofs that allow rainwater to run off rather than puddle.

A gazebo is relatively easy to set up. With a little practice, you should be able to do it yourself in a few minutes. Until you have money to invest in a more solid alternative, gazebos are not a bad choice. They get the job done.

Pole Tents

These are another viable option for crafters. Pole tents are just what they say they are—tents constructed from horizontal and vertical poles connected by a network of "Y," "V" and "X" joints. The poles are usually thick and strong, making the pole tent sturdy and stable. Note: The weak points of a pole tent are where the poles are inserted into the joints. These can come apart if not properly secured. If you buy a pole tent, *always* remember to lock the poles securely into the joints. The hardware to do this is included with each joint.

Prices for a complete 10′ × 10′ pole tent package start at about $200. You can also buy the joints and poles separately. The complete package as well as individual components are sold at most large flea markets and outdoor specialty markets. The poles can be found (and cut to your specifications) at most hardware and home remodeling stores.

Unlike canopy tents, pole tents do require assembly. This takes a little

Pole tents come in a variety of designs: *flat* roof, *slanted* roof and *peaked* roof are just a few. Don't buy any design that would allow rainwater to collect or puddle on the tent top. A peaked roof is best.

practice. You can master assembly more easily if you code each pole and corresponding connector with a permanent market. Then, each time you set it up, just follow your own directions.

The beauty of a pole tent is that the size can be changed and adapted easily to any show space size. This is not true of the gazebo or canopy tents. The size of a pole tent is dictated by the length of the poles. The *design* is dictated by the type of joints you use to connect them. This flexibility opens a world of possibilities for a crafter. Your pole tent can be used as a protective covering at outdoor shows as well as a display frame for indoor showing—no matter what the space size—simply by using longer or shorter poles. If you use your tent frame for indoor showing, a pole tent is the only way to go. If you hang heavy products or display equipment from your tent, a pole tent is the best choice. It's designed to take the weight.

Canopy Tents

These all-in-one tents are the most popular choice of crafters. The frame is constructed somewhat like an accordion—all the poles and supports are preattached to one another via a network of aluminum trusses. No real assembly is required. You take the tent out of the case, gradually expand the tent to its full size, add the top and you're done! With a little practice, you can erect a canopy tent in a short period of time.

Most canopy tents are much heavier than either the dining canopy or the gazebo but not quite as strong as a good pole tent. And having the entire frame construction attached to itself means you can't carry it in sections—it's all or nothing. Most people don't find it too heavy to manage. It's even easier to handle if you buy the carrying case.

Canopy tents are made with the crafter in mind. The tops are peaked, the side curtains can be secured, and they are constructed of water-resistant fabric that meets most fire/safety codes. And they are available in our favorite color—white.

Canopy tents are ten feet square—the exact size of the average crafts show booth (other sizes are also available). Guylines and ground stakes need not extend far (if at all) from the tent itself. They can be hung almost straight down from the corners of the canopy, thus taking up less overall space. Canopy tents hold up well under most weather conditions, better than gazebos and dining canopies. What more could you ask for?

Canopy tents are also a great deal more expensive than other types of tents—about $500 more or less. The side curtains are an additional $250 or so. But the superior construction of the canopy tent makes it an excellent and convenient choice for most crafters.

Dining Canopies

Though a dining canopy may work fine on a camping trip or in your backyard (the purpose for which it was intended), it doesn't work very well as a protective covering for your crafts show display. A dining canopy is really nothing more than a square piece of green plastic held up by five very wobbly metal poles, one for each corner and one straight up the center.

The green plastic dining canopy will not enhance the color of your products. It will cast a dark shadow over your display and not allow enough light to filter through. Having a pole in the middle of your booth will be a nuisance to you *and* your customers.

The guylines and stakes necessary to stabilize a dining canopy must stretch quite a distance from the tent itself to spread the top so it doesn't sag. The distance may exceed your allotted show space and infringe another crafter's territory. You must constantly adjust the tension ropes to keep the canopy top tight and smooth, but your efforts will be in vain. The top and sides will still sag into your display. Rainwater will also puddle precariously on the top of the tent surface even though it is slightly peaked. When too much water accumulates, it will create a waterfall effect that your customers will not appreciate. In a strong wind, it will be virtually impossible to keep your dining canopy erect and stable.

Dining canopies don't work at all when displaying on hard surfaces such as blacktop or cement because there is no feasible way to anchor them securely without driving stakes into the ground, which is usually not permitted on hard surfaces.

The only good thing I can say about dining canopies is that they are cheap—about $25. Which is why I mention them here. Many new crafters, having limited funds and gearing up for their first outdoor show, may be tempted to purchase them. If it's your *only* option, it's better than nothing.

Anchoring Your Tent

Display tents are potentially dangerous equipment that require responsible management. Wind—even if it isn't a strong wind—can pick your tent up and blow it away. Let's do some visual imaging here. Think of your tent as a fifty- to seventy-five-pound kite with a wing span of ten feet. Now picture it flying through the air at a crafts show filled with hundreds of people, thousands of pieces of breakable product and rows of other tents. Scary, isn't it? So, do the right thing—secure your tent.

How do you do this? Most crafters use ropes or elastic bungee cords

To securely anchor your tent, use two sets of weights or ground stakes per corner of your tent. If you use weights, make sure they are heavy enough. One ten-pound weight per corner will only make your tent that much heavier and more dangerous should it become unanchored. Try more like fifty pounds per corner.

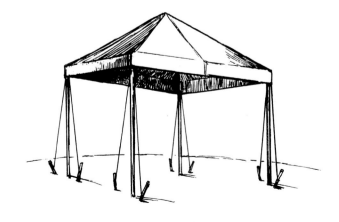

attached to the top structure of their tents and anchored to the ground with metal or plastic stakes. This is a relatively safe way to anchor your tent. Use two sets of ropes and stakes per tent corner.

Another way to anchor your tent is with weights attached by rope from the tent structure to the ground. But all too often the weights used are not heavy enough to really hold the tent down. One ten-pound weight at each corner will just make your tent that much heavier and more dangerous as it flies through the air. Try more like fifty pounds per corner.

Some crafters use buckets filled with hardened cement to weigh their tents down. In the center of the cement is a pipe in which the vertical pole of the tent is inserted. This is an inexpensive solution that usually works just fine. If the bucket is large enough, the cement will be heavy enough to keep your tent on the ground under most wind conditions. Make sure the tent pole is secured in the pipe so it can't slip out. Drill holes in the pipe and the pole, and slide a screw through both of them.

If you hang display hardware (such as lattice) directly from your tent frame, that will also add weight to the tent and keep it from moving. But don't count on it as the only means of anchoring your tent. More weight is still needed.

Sandbags and cement blocks, attached securely to the tent frame, are also used quite often. These, I believe, are not heavy enough to keep your

Cement-filled buckets, sandbags and cement blocks, fixed to the tent with ropes or bungee cords, will help your tent stay anchored to the ground. Don't be lulled into a false sense of security just because it is a nice day with a gentle breeze; even a light breeze can pick your tent off the ground. Anchor your tent as soon as it is erected.

tent from moving in a good wind. Double up on them—two sets per tent corner.

How you secure your tent will depend partly on what type of surface you are displaying on. For grass and soil, any of the above will work, though I recommend ropes and plenty of stakes. These take up a minimum of storage room. On blacktop and cement, you can't hammer anything into the ground so stakes are out of the question. You have no choice but to use weights.

Protecting Your Hardware and Software

Wind, rain and even heat can do irreparable damage to the very foundations of your display—your hardware and software. Wood can age unevenly and prematurely. Fabrics can fade and sustain permanent water damage. Metal hardware and software can pit and rust. Shelving units, racks, tables, tablecovers, lattice and other equipment should be protected against the elements.

Moisture

Your tent will, most of the time, shield your display pieces, but not always and not entirely. There will be instances when you have to set up and break down your display in the rain, when a canopy or side curtain breaks loose and the rain filters in, when it is just so darn humid outside that a layer of moisture seems to permeate everything. Untreated wood should at least be sealed to protect it. Apply a coat of polyeurethane or other sealant to keep it looking nice.

Moisture can also take its toll on your fabric tablecovers and fabric-covered software. Many fabrics are just not moisture-friendly. Suede, velvet, taffeta and satin (just to name a few) do not fare well. They may develop water spots that are not easily removed. Dry clean them immediately. Cottons and other natural fabrics wrinkle and pucker. Avoid fragile fabrics and look for synthetic easy-care look-alike, feel-alike alternatives.

Metal is another medium that can be adversely affected by moisture.

Surface imperfections are an open invitation to rust. If metal hardware gets wet from rain or humidity, dry it immediately.

Wind

Wind can also do substantial damage to your hardware and software—and ultimately to your product. At many outdoor shows, you will use your tent frame and top without side curtains, subjecting your products and hardware to anything from gentle breezes to strong gusts of wind. How will you keep your hardware from toppling to the ground with your products on it? How will you prevent small tabletop hardware from blowing off the table? How will you keep your table coverings from blowing up and over your product?

There are many ways to stabilize your display equipment. For the large display pieces, homemade sandbags are a simple solution. Cut the legs off an old pair of jeans, fill them with sand, dirt or small pebbles and close the ends. Lay them across the bottom rung of U-shaped table legs, drape them over the base of your shelving unit, use them almost anywhere. It's an inexpensive solution that works fairly well.

Your large display hardware can also be attached to your tent poles with bungee cords or rope. This will not only keep your hardware from falling over, it will add more weight and stability to your tent.

Rope and tent stakes work fine for anchoring hardware. Drape the rope over an inconspicuous part of your display (the base or bottom shelf) and stake it to the ground. Do not use bungee cords—they stretch too much. Add weight to all smaller hardware or you may spend the entire show day running after it! If you make it yourself, use bricks or solid wood blocks as the base.

If you protect your hardware and software from the damages of wind, sun and rain, you will protect your products as well.

Adapting Your Indoor Display for Outdoor Use

Selling crafts is a tough and often inconvenient business. Selling at outdoor shows can be even more so. Not only do you have to pack and lug your products and hardware from show to show, but when selling outdoors you have the added responsibility of packing, setting up, securing and breaking down tent equipment.

When I first started selling at outdoor shows, I brought all of the same equipment that I used when selling indoors *plus* the tent, weights and so on. After a few shows, I said to myself, "There *must* be a better way to do this." And there was.

Your tent does not have to be an added piece of equipment. Depending on what you sell, it can often be used as a substitute for some of your larger, more cumbersome hardware. You may be able to hang or support smaller and lighter hardware from your tent frame rather than transporting all of your large, free-standing display equipment.

Check the "closet organizer" section of your local general merchandise store for display options (shelving units, gridwalls, etc.) that can hang from a closet pole. If it can hang from a *closet* pole, it can hang from your *tent frame* just as well. A simple solution that works well for fabric and clothing items is to tie dowels with clean white rope (or chain) to make "ladders" to hang product from.

I'll use my own display as an example. For an indoor 10′ × 10′ booth, I pack eight five-foot wooden shelves, four wood display supports, four wooden ladders *plus* four wooden stands and an assortment of wood dowels. That's just the display hardware. Add to that my *product*, and my station wagon is really packed!

For an outdoor 10′ × 10′ display, I only bring *one* shelving unit, lots of rope or chain, wood dowels and my tent equipment. That's all. Why? Because I use my tent (which takes up less space) as a substitute for three large pieces of display hardware. I have so much extra room in my car that sometimes I even bring booth carpet—and always more product.

Outdoor shows can be fun. Given the choice, I would rather spend a day in the great outdoors (no matter what the weather) than enclosed in a stuffy room. Plan and prepare yourself well, and outdoor selling can be successful.

Commercial Displays

If you decide to broaden your selling market, consider displaying your products in a commercial/retail environment. Whether you choose a crafts mall, gift shop, consignment shop or almost any other retail establishment, it would be wise whenever possible to provide your own display equipment.

Providing Stores with Ready-Made Displays

Many manufacturers prefer to use their own display equipment when selling in a retail environment. It is a common practice. Go to any department store, card shop, gift or general merchandise store. You will see many freestanding displays provided by the manufacturer. Why? Because, in most cases, no one knows better than you how to showcase your products so they will sell.

If you were to sell or consign the earrings you make to a gift shop, the store owner might put them in an enclosed case or in an area away from customer view. But if you provided your own display apparatus, such as a revolving counter or floor display, many of your wholesale accounts would use the display you provided. *If* it didn't take up too much space. *If* it was

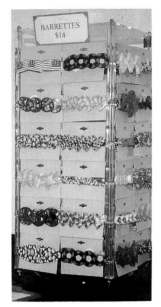

A compact, self-contained display such as this jewelry carousel, showcases a large amount of product in a very small area. Retailers like that. Design your own commercial display wherever possible. Don't leave it up to the retailer who may or may not know the best way to showcase your particular product.

commercially acceptable. *If* it was aesthetically pleasing.

Instead of your jewelry being consigned to a shelf somewhere on aisle number three or in a case under reflective glass, the store might put your compact revolving display right on the counter close to the cash register, a very advantageous place—the perfect location for impulse-buying. Your sales would be much better because your products would have more exposure.

Customers spend between two to ten minutes at a store's cash register. They wait while the sale is tallied. They wait while credit card approval is completed. They wait while their purchases are packaged or wrapped. These delays provide more time for customers to look at your products. The more they look, the better the chance they will buy. Now, whether or not the retailer puts your products right next to the cash register is up to them. But if your products are small and you can provide a self-contained display, there's a good possibility your products might be displayed in that very advantageous location.

Retail space is expensive. When you design a commercial display, you want to put a substantial sampling and a decent quantity of product in a small amount of space without crowding them. Sound impossible? Really, it isn't. You can make an efficient, professional, eye-catching and reasonably priced commercial display.

At some crafts co-ops, you pay for the amount of space you use to display your product. The less space you use, the lower the price—a strong incentive to make the most of the smallest space possible without sacrificing product visibility (and sales) for economy.

In other commercial settings, your products might be mixed in with a host of other merchandise. It would be advantageous to make sure all of your products were grouped together. It makes for a better showing. Using your own display would guarantee that.

A retail display should be:

1. compact

2. simple

3. aesthetically pleasing

4. commercially acceptable

Compact and Simple

You should be able to fit a considerable amount and variety of products on or in your commercial display without making it too large. Spatial economy is the key. Use air space rather than wall or floor space.

Also, the larger and more complicated your display apparatus, the more expensive it will probably be to make or buy. If you are servicing more than one store, you will need a display apparatus for each store. This could get very expensive. You could charge the store a rental fee for the display if it is large, expensive, elaborate and necessary, but it *is* most often advantageous to show your own products on your own display equipment. Too high a rental fee, or in some cases, any rental fee at all, might discourage a small store owner from using your equipment.

To make the best use of commercial space, the display apparatus should provide product visibility on more than one side.

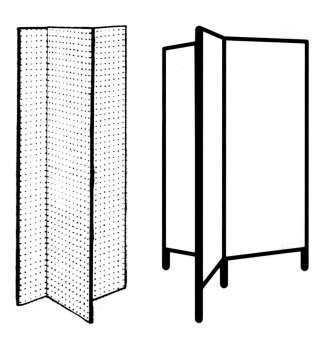

To make the best use of space, the display apparatus should provide product visibility on more than one side if possible. If the customer has access to only one side, a revolving display would work best.

Height is another issue. From the retailer's standpoint, a display with some height is better than a wide display. Use more air space rather than counter or shelf space. Your retailer will thank you.

For my products, my commercial display consists of a few wooden dowels and some clean white rope (a variation of my outdoor display design). Now, this may sound too simple, but it is very effective. It is not expensive to make and it displays my products just as I want it to.

My display is usually suspended from the ceiling, utilizing space that otherwise may have remained vacant. Retailers like that. It can be one-dimensional (flat against a wall), two-dimensional (in an aisle and viewed from both sides) or three- or four-dimensional (hung in the center of a room and visible from three or four sides).

Sometimes you can duplicate the same type of display equipment for commercial selling that you use at crafts shows. In other cases, you will have to design a more compact and scaled-down version of your crafts show display. In yet other situations, the store's displays will work just as well for your products as any you could devise. If this is true, use their display equipment and save yourself some money. It depends on the product. It depends on how much inventory you choose to show and how much space the retailer agrees to give you.

Spatial economy is the key—for commercial displays as well as for crafts show displays. This three-board presentation, when slightly creased or hinged at the seams, takes up less space on a wall, crafts show table or retail counter than if it were displayed flat.

Aesthetically Pleasing

Whatever the mechanics of your particular display, make it neat and pleasing to look at. This doesn't mean it must be decorated or ornate, but it should fit into the selling environment and harmonize with the decor. Your display should mesh with the *flavor* of the store. A glass and chrome display in a country gift shop will simply scream, "I don't belong here!"

Your display should also echo the flavor of your craft and products whenever possible—old-looking stuff displayed in an antique setting, new stuff in a modern setting. Handmade quilts displayed on metal rods or racks, or art deco glass pieces on rustic shelving just doesn't look right.

Commercially Acceptable

Your display, while showcasing your products, should also be commercially acceptable. That is, it should look *professional*. The apparatus should be sturdy and well made. A store owner will not be pleased to have your display coming unglued or falling apart. It is not their job to rescrew, reglue and maintain your equipment. They have more important things to do, like selling your products.

The products themselves must fit securely on the display yet permit customer access. Customers may want to remove them for closer inspection. Many more customers will handle your display and your products in a commercial setting than at crafts shows. Your products will be on display five to seven days a week. Make your display capable of withstanding the added stress of constant use—and abuse.

Craft- and Product-Specific Commercial Displays

The larger your product, the more difficult it may be to display and the more limited the number of pieces you will be able to show at one time. The smaller the product, the greater your displaying options.

Small Products

Any small product has a good chance of ending up on the sales counter if you display it properly—jewelry in revolving cases, miniatures in shadow-boxes, wood cutouts or blocks in a rustic organizer, ornaments on a small tree, rosebuds and other individual flowers in a decorative vase, pen and ink gift cards in a literature holder, a rubber stamp display, belt buckles—are all good candidates for countertop displaying. The smaller the product, the more you need to provide your own self-contained display for it. Tiny items can be lost by retailers and overlooked by customers.

Medium-Size Products

Most crafts products fall into this category. Medium-size products are more readily visible than smaller products just because of size. Freestanding products are often most comfortably displayed on shelves. Clothing and fabric crafts are more easily seen if they are hung for display purposes. Artwork and hanging florals most often require wall space. For the sake of spatial economy, freestanding product "trees" are another acceptable display medium for midsize products.

PRODUCTS DISPLAYED ON SHELVES

If your midsize products display best on shelves, most likely you can use the retailer's shelves instead of providing your own display. Dolls, wooden toys, carousels, pottery, ceramics, candles, freestanding floral arrangements and flower pots are just some of the crafts products most likely displayed on shelves.

PRODUCTS THAT HANG

For fabric products that hang, painted or stained wood dowels often work best. The heavier the product, the thicker the dowel should be. Metal gridwalls with extensions from which hangers can be hung are another, though more expensive, option for clothing. These can be freestanding or wall-mounted. Hang florals from pegboard or lattice displays.

PRODUCTS THAT REQUIRE WALL SPACE

Wall space is at a premium in a retail selling environment. There are only so many walls available. And wall space is only one-sided. Consider a three-sided (or four) freestanding type of display rather than expecting the retailer to give up precious wall space. These are compact and provide a good deal of display space in a limited area.

Very Large Products

These are the most difficult products to place in a retail environment. Like wall space, floor space is also at a premium. Your best chance might be a new gift shop (if that suits your product) or any *new* shop. Owners might not yet have sufficient inventory to fill the store to capacity. They might welcome your large products to fill empty space and increase their selection of products.

If retailers are going to give up valuable floor space to a large product, they will expect a handsome return on that product. Otherwise it would not be worth their while. Large, expensive products have a better chance at being accepted by a retailer than large inexpensive products.

Selling through retail stores is a convenient way to do business. Your products will have constant and consistent exposure, six or seven days a week. It's a great supplement to crafts show selling, but it also requires additional inventory and possibly additional display equipment, which can get expensive. If you have the time to stockpile some inventory, if you have the money to build or buy compact and efficient commercial display equipment, it can be very worthwhile.

Part Three

SALESMANSHIP

What Is Salesmanship?

In the first two parts of this book, we talked about quiet hints and subliminal messages to help your customers see and appreciate the value of you and your work. But so far, the marketing techniques we've employed have been subtle.

Though you might argue that having a feature article and your photograph appear in a newspaper may not seem subtle, it really is. You were not asking for an immediate response. You were not pressing anyone to make a decision. You were not facing the public directly—and expectantly—with hope of a sale obviously shining in your eyes.

By communicating these subtle hints and subliminal messages, you were laying the groundwork and building some momentum toward the final step—the sale itself. Now you are ready to face your customers and wow them with your very presence.

Think of it as building a house. The foundation was laid with market research and your carefully designed choice of products. Then you framed and reinforced the structure with your image-building skills. Great care has been taken to decorate your environment. And now, you will actually have to live in the house you built. Now you can start inviting guests, your customers, into your home. But first, let's fine-tune your hostessing skills.

How do you want your customers to *feel* when they enter your domain? You want them to enjoy the experience. So let's make them comfortable . . . let's put them at ease . . . let's make them glad they came.

And let's not let them walk away empty-handed. Let's sell them something.

Dealing face to face with customers for the first time can be a daunting experience. After all, you are asking them to buy something from you. Nobody likes to do that. And what if they said "no"?

The whole concept of hawking your wares can also seem somehow demeaning. And when customers don't buy your products, you may even feel a little embarrassed and certainly disappointed. But don't feel that way. Look at it in a different light for a moment. View selling not so much as *asking* but more as *offering* and, even, *helping.*

Though some people go to a crafts show to browse or to copy what is on display, most go for only one reason—to buy. And they are as anxious to buy as you are to sell. So you are not asking them to do anything they don't want to do. You are helping them by giving them choices. Feel better?

Selling is hard work. And being an effective salesman takes a little practice. Salesmanship is a combination of knowledge and diplomacy. The knowledge part—knowing your customers, the industry and your particular craft and product market—will give you confidence in yourself and what you are selling. The "diplomacy" part is a little trickier.

We are all salesmen in one way or another and have been for most of our lives, though perhaps before we started selling crafts we had never been *product* salesmen. But at some point in your life, you have tried to sell someone something. It may have been an idea. You may have tried to persuade someone to think as you do. Perhaps you tried to sway a friend or spouse to see one movie instead of another. In this situation, you were trying to sell them on your idea. You were trying to show them the *value* of it. Sometimes you used gentle persuasion; at other times, you probably came right out and asked for what you wanted. The basics are the same no matter what you are selling—a product or an idea.

In this section we will focus on the sales process itself—the personal exchange between customer and crafter. The contact point. The encounter, if you will. What to do and what not to do at a show. What to say and what not to say to a customer. Let's look at what to do first, since your customers will see you before they actually get to speak with you.

What to Do

Many crafters feel awkward at a crafts show, waiting for customers but not wanting to *look* as though you are waiting for customers. Do I sit or do I stand? Do I make eye contact? Do I twiddle my thumbs until they ask for help? Let's take some of the guesswork out of what to do at a crafts show.

The key, first of all, is to look busy—but not too busy. You don't want to appear as though you are sitting or standing in your booth just waiting to pounce on the first customer who comes along. Nor do you want to look so intensely occupied in an activity that a customer would feel awkward interrupting you. How do you communicate to your customers that you are not waiting for them, but that you *are* ready to help them?

Body Language

Words are not the only form of communication. Your body has a language of its own that sends some very powerful messages to your customers. Use it to convey the *right* messages.

If you stood in the center of your show booth, staring ahead, with arms folded across your chest and your legs spread in a defensive stance, all you would be missing is an Uzi machine gun. The perception would be of someone ready to ward off an attack. No sane customer would enter your booth to challenge you.

But, if you were casually adjusting your product, and looking up now and then to acknowledge and speak with your customers, your body language would say, "I may look busy, but I always have time for you. I am receptive to you. I *like* you and I am here to help you."

Be careful of body language that may be misinterpreted. Too big a smile might seem like you are eager to sell—perhaps too eager. Staring at a customer might be interpreted as a challenge. If you don't smile at all, customers may think you are in a bad mood.

Potential customers will see you long before they have a chance to talk to you. It will do you no good to "light up" only when in conversation. Your initial body language may turn customers away before you can make verbal contact.

When a customer is in your show booth, don't invade their personal space. Every person has a perimeter defense line and most feel uncomfortable when it is violated. Stand as close as you need to, but not too close. This is a *business* relationship. You are not their mother or their best friend. Don't touch your customers (pat them on the back, etc.). These are blatant violations of their personal space.

Hurried motions are another "no, no." Give the impression you have all day to spend with each customer, while actually devoting only enough time to make a sale and to satisfy their needs. Slow, deliberate movements are perceived as those of an organized and competent individual. Quick, frenetic actions give the opposite impression.

The messages you convey with your body are powerful sales tools. Avoid any action that may be negatively interpreted by your customers. *Do* use body language to communicate positive and encouraging messages. What you do is as important as what you say.

Reading Customer Signals

Your body is not the only one sending out signals. Your customers will be communicating also through their own body language. Learn to read them accurately, and you'll never miss a sale.

This doesn't mean every person who enters your show booth will buy something—they won't. But by being able to identify those who *probably* will, or those who *want* to, you can devote your time and best efforts to interacting with these people rather than spending too much time on someone who probably *won't* buy anything.

How would you read a customer who walks into your booth, obviously afraid to make eye contact? Would you assume that they are thinking of stealing something? That they looked somehow guilty?

Well, the only thing they might be guilty of is the fact that they have no intention of buying your products. Their body language is telling you *not* to make contact with them yet. They only came to browse, not to buy. Though later they may decide to purchase something, right now they definitely don't want to talk to you. Don't scare them away. Let them browse until it looks like they are interested in something.

On the other hand, someone who walks purposefully into your booth and immediately makes eye contact may be *ready* to buy. Perhaps they have seen your products before and already know what they want. Don't ignore them. Contact immediately, even if all you can say is, "I'll be with you in a moment." Of course, their purpose may be simply to ask you pleadingly where the ladies' room is, but they obviously did have a purpose.

If a customer looks but doesn't touch, or walks through your booth with their hands clasped behind their backs, they are probably afraid that if they even *touch* something, you'll make them buy it. Put them at ease. Acknowledge their presence, but don't move toward them.

If a customer shows interest, picks up or dwells on a particular product, then it is time to connect. Now, don't get too excited and rush over to them. They might put it down and rush just as quickly to the door. S-l-o-w-l-y turn and either casually give them more information or ask if they need any help.

Your customers will give you many different signals just by the way they enter your booth, clutch their pocketbooks, avert their eyes, acknowledge you or ignore you. Some of their body language will give you mixed signals—probably because they themselves are not sure what they are going to do. Study your customers. Learn the signals that will result in sales.

What You Should and Should Not Be Doing

When a customer comes abreast of your show booth, make preliminary eye contact with them. Don't stare—that will intimidate them. Don't prolong the look, willing them to come into your booth—that will challenge and pressure them. Just look up, acknowledge their presence, say a quick "hello" with your eyes and *smile*. If they seem at all hesitant, go back to whatever it is you were doing. Don't move in on them.

These actions will convey the following messages:

eye contact = "I acknowledge your presence"

smile = "Welcome! I'm glad to be here and I'm glad you're here too"

returning to your activity = "I'm not going to pressure, but I am here if you need me."

Smiling (not a wide toothy grin, just a turning up of the corners of your mouth) is something you should do a lot of at a crafts show. Just repeat over and over to yourself "I *love* this! And I'm happy to be here."

Don't hide behind a screen or partition. There's nothing to be afraid of. *Do* make yourself visible and accessible to your customers. They should not have to look for you. Position yourself where they can see you.

Face toward your customers and not away from them. Though you may have to turn away now and then, don't maintain this pose for long periods of time. Face them to show them you are approachable and receptive to them.

Don't rush toward a customer as soon as they enter your booth. Customers feel intimidated when they see a crafter poised, obviously ready to pounce when they themselves have not yet made any decisions to buy.

Don't focus too intently on your customers. Give them a little space. Let them browse a while on their own, but not for too long.

Do speak with them casually while doing something else, unless their actions request that you attend to them. They will show you with their body language what they need from you.

Do something! Straighten or rearrange some product. Polish it. Dust it. Fold it. Unfold it. Complete a work-in-progress. Do anything so you don't look idle or bored. Don't make it look as though you are still setting up your booth, but do make yourself look useful.

Often, when you go to a crafts show, you see crafters taking the opposite tack. They sit in a quiet corner, reading a book. Don't do this! The customers are left to fend for themselves. The crafter offers no information and no encouragement. She reads on, waiting for a customer to interrupt her with a sale. "Interrupt" is the key word here. You are forcing your customers to do something they have been taught not to do—to interrupt.

You are also putting your sales in jeopardy. Many customers will walk away, though a few might interrupt you. Reading a book instead of being a salesperson is not only unproductive, it is actually detrimental to your sales. Remember, you are not a disinterested party—you are there to *sell*. Though some products will be sold with little or no effort on your part, most sales will be the result of interaction between you and your customer. They may require some information or need some hand-holding and reassurance. It is your job to give them whatever they need. Every sale counts. Save the book for later—as a reward for having a great day of sales.

Where to Stand and Sit

Sit rarely; stand mostly. The only exception would be if you are demonstrating your craft technique or attending to a work-in-progress. Then it's okay to sit.

Sometimes, you will have very little to say about where you sit or stand. The size of your show space and how you must position your display equipment will dictate it. Try always to give yourself at least a small corner of your own. Use your sales area to get out of your customers' way and still remain accessible.

If you are too far removed from your customers, it will be difficult to help them. If you are too far removed from your product, it will be difficult to keep an eye on it. Situate yourself where you can easily attend to both your customers and your product.

Try not to block yourself in and away from the customers' section of your show booth. Sometimes this is difficult, especially if you display on tables. A show booth filled with three tables doesn't leave much room for you to move around. And your best position will probably be on one side of the tables while customers will be on the other. Still, try to leave yourself a path to get to all areas of your display—just in case.

Since my display materials occupy only the perimeter of my show booth, I have access to my customers as well as my products. There is a large interior area where I can stand. But if I were to place myself dead center in that area, I would look very eager indeed. So I don't do that. Sometimes I sit in my sales area and attend to minor paperwork or stitch a work-in-progress. What I do most of the time is stand by my display—folding and unfolding my product.

What to Do to Draw Attention

Folding and unfolding product serves a dual purpose. First of all, it helps me look busy. Second, it offers customers a full view of each product as I remove it from the rack, shake it out, lay it out and refold it.

This is a good marketing technique for bringing your products to the customers' attention. If it's a toy, play with it. If it's a fabric item, fold and unfold it. If it's a floral piece, rearrange it. If it's a jewelry item, put it on and take it off. If it's a music box, play it. Whatever your product, experiment with different ways to show it off without seeming to do so.

Demonstrating a craft technique is another excellent way to draw attention to your products and craft. Customers are always fascinated by the how-to's of what you make. If your craft process involves potentially dangerous materials, equipment or techniques, always check first with the show producer for fire/safety restrictions that may apply. If you anticipate demonstrating your craft often or consistently throughout the duration of the show, bring another person to write up sales slips and help sell your product. It's difficult to demonstrate *and* sell at the same time.

How to Handle More Than One Customer at a Time

Believe it or not, it is not difficult to handle more than one customer at a time. Don't become panicked or nervous if several customers in your booth are competing for your attention at the same time. Take each one individually and in turn. Find out what each one wants. Some questions can be dispatched quickly—to be followed up in a minute or two. Others will take longer. Satisfy the easy ones first. One customer may only want to know the price of an item (having your product price-marked would avoid this). You should know the price by heart. Tell her. Another will want to know if the product comes in a different size or color. That you should be able to answer quickly. But you may be able to show her something else that meets her needs (and you don't want her to walk away) so say, "I'll be able to help you in a minute," or point her in the direction of the product she is looking for.

Your first priority is completing the sale. Answer the questions that can be answered quickly, delay those that can't, but first and foremost take care of those customers who have already made the decision to purchase.

Your Final Moments With Your Customer

These are important moments. Don't rush them. Your final moments with a purchasing customer will not only set the stage for future purchases, it will be the last memory your customer has of you. Package your product neatly and lovingly, showing one last time that you value the product you just sold her. This will reinforce the message that your customer has made a good choice.

I usually run my hands slowly over the fabric to smooth out any wrinkles, then I carefully place tissue paper between the folds before placing in into a bag. This is very effective. Package your products in a nice way. Don't hurry this final process. If you do, your customer will feel as though you just want to be rid of her. This is not the image you want your customer to remember.

Leave each customer on a warm and personal note. Communicate that you hope she will be happy with the purchase . . . that you hope her sister will like it . . . that it will look just lovely with her new couch. Let her know you have been *listening* to her and not just that you are glad to have sold her something.

What to Say

This is where many crafters have the most difficulty—*talking* to their customers. We've all been in situations where we pleasantly addressed a customer, only to have them smile back—blankly or self-consciously—and then walk away. There will always be customers who do this. Don't let that discourage you from making contact. You didn't do anything wrong. It is your *job* to make verbal contact with them.

 Speak to your customers . . .

- *First*, to establish a connection
- *Second*, to develop a rapport
- *Third*, to make a sale

To Speak or Not to Speak

Always say *something*. Though your first few attempts at speaking with your customers might not produce the results you had expected, say something anyway. It is, most of the time, better to speak than not to speak.

When you talk to customers, your need to sell them something should not be blatantly apparent. The customer already knows why you are there. Speak first to make a connection and to develop a rapport, *then* to make a sale.

How to Develop a Rapport With Your Customer

Find some common ground, something to elicit a response and not make your customer feel in any way pressed or uncomfortable—just a little conversation between two people.

Making a Statement

One way to establish common ground is to make a nonthreatening statement with which your customer can identify. But since it is not posed as a question, you may or may not get any kind of response.

If you were to say, "That's a lovely pocketbook you have," that is a statement. Most likely, your customer will provide you with more information about the pocketbook, "Thanks, my mom gave it to me for my birthday." They might also just say, "Thank you," and walk away.

Suppose you took a sniff of air and said, "Mmmmm, the florals make it smell so nice in here!" What do you think your customer's response might be? Could you develop a conversation from that?

Your statement can be something very general about the weather or perhaps your surroundings. You could focus on something more personal, such as your customer's clothing, or children. But you are still only *hoping* that they will respond to you and that after the initial contact you will be able to continue the dialogue. Statements don't guarantee continued conversation.

A statement that might be more worthwhile is one in answer to a query or observation that one customer might make to another and that you might overhear. (Yes, eavesdropping is allowed at crafts shows.) You could learn quite a bit from your customers if you listen to their conversations.

You might overhear one customer saying to another, "It's freezing in here!" Don't miss the opportunity to jump in and say, "I'm a little cold myself," even though the statement wasn't posed directly to you. No one will mind and you will be establishing common ground and opening the lines of communication by agreeing with them.

If you overhear a customer saying, "I wonder if this product is machine-washable," or anything else about your products, don't hesitate to casually supply an answer.

Asking a Question

Questions are far more valuable than statements in developing a rapport with your customers. They encourage two-way conversation. A question, in polite society, *demands* a response.

The question can be something formulated to contribute to your customer profile ("Are you more partial to silver or gold jewelry?"). It can be a personal question ("Where did you get that pocketbook—I just love it!"), or it can just be a way of making small talk ("Is it raining outside?").

I try to design my questions to learn more about my customers—their wants and needs. As long as I'm going to ask a question, it might as well be one that will provide me with useful information. Small talk is nice, and if you feel more comfortable making initial conversation with your customers this way, then go ahead. If your customer is just browsing, then small talk may be just what you need to bring them a little closer and make them relax. If your customer touches, tries on or picks up any of your products, move past the small talk and on to the subject at hand—your products. And do it in the form of a question.

Tell Them Something Interesting

By answering a question, the customer is giving *you* information. Now it's time to return the favor and give *them* some information—about yourself, your products and materials, and about your craft.

Be careful when imparting information about yourself to your customers. Neither boast or brag. They don't want to know your life story either. Just tell them the good points as a matter of fact, subtly in conversation.

As for your products, you're allowed to do a little bragging, as long as it is peppered with some hard information. Tell your customers what makes your products special. Tell them about the high-quality raw materials used to create them. Mention (without complaining) how long it took to make each one. List different uses for it. Emphasize the positive features of your product.

When it comes to your craft, your customers might be interested in a brief history of the craft itself. They may want to know how long you have been working at your craft. You could briefly describe the steps necessary to make a particular product—or the craft process employed to make all of your products.

These interesting facts will help you sell. They are reinforcing, in your customers' minds, the *value* of your work. You are giving them a reason to buy.

Other Ways to Develop a Rapport

There will be times when your main objective will be just to get your customers to smile. A happy customer is a more receptive customer.

One crafter constantly told short but very funny jokes as he went about dealing with his customers. The impression was of someone who was just glad to be there. Sales were almost secondary. He was so jovial that his customers were all smiling and laughing as they left his show booth—with their purchases. This crafter laughed all the way to the bank. Most of us could not carry this off successfully. We wouldn't have his timing nor his delivery. But it worked very well for him.

The point is, don't take selling so seriously that you don't enjoy it and that your customers won't enjoy it either. Your customer will not think you unprofessional if you make a witty (or even downright funny) comment now and then. They will be grateful for it. Life is too short not to have laughter.

Another way to develop rapport is to empathize with a customer's comment and to follow that with a short, interesting story of your own. *Customer*= "My mother tried to make one of these . . ." *Crafter*= "When I first started making them, I did the same thing . . . But one day . . ."

After a few years (even months) in the crafts business, you'll have plenty of stories to tell!

Through the years, I have formulated a scenario that often begins with small talk, followed closely by asking some important questions, and eventually gearing my customers toward products I know will fill their needs.

Here's the beginning of one possible conversation:

Me (sniffing the air) = "It sure smells like Christmas in here, doesn't it?" or "Don't you just *love* the scent of cinnamon and cloves?"

Customer = "I just love everything about this season!"

Me = "I especially like *decorating* for the season. What kind of Christmas tree do you have—real or artificial?"

The salesmanship begins . . .

Don't spend all of your time "visiting" with just one customer. Hopefully, you'll have more than one at a time in your booth. These conversations need to be as condensed as possible without seeming to be so.

To avoid repetition, speak loudly and clearly enough so other customers in your booth will hear your conversations and the information you are imparting to one customer. Keep an eye out for what you say to one that may interest another. For example, I might tell a customer that, "My tree skirts range from very small tabletop size to several that would comfortably fit a fifteen-foot tree." If I see another customer perk up as I say "fifteen-foot tree," I'd show the very large tree skirt for just a second. Nine times out of ten, the second customer will come over and pull it out. More often than not, they will end up buying it. Meanwhile, I will be showing my present customer what would suit *her*. Once she makes a decision. I would go on to that second customer.

At a Crafts Show . . .

Speak to your customers—always say *something*.

- Make a statement
- Ask a question
- Provide information
- Relate a story
- Say something funny!

Key Words That Can Help Boost Your Sales

First, I'd like to share what key words will *not* boost your sales. Don't pressure a customer by telling them, "This is the last one" of an item. That's a high-pressure tactic today's wary customers do not appreciate. If it is truly the last piece of a particular product, will you/can you make any more? Then there's no need to threaten them with this statement. If you can't make any more (such as a limited-edition piece) then say it *casually*, not pointedly. And follow the statement up with something positive, ". . . But I'll have a new series coming out next year."

Don't threaten them with price increases either. "This is a special show price. After today, the price will go up"—another high-pressure tactic that usually backfires. Anything and everything you say to your customers should be *positive*.

Tell them something that will make them *want* to purchase rather than making them afraid *not* to purchase. Phrases (*true* phrases) such as "original design," "one-of-a-kind," "heirloom quality," "the very best materials," "collectible" and "popular" are just a few key words and phrases that will help you sell. Let's see how you could infuse them into your conversations:

"This is an *original design* and my most *popular* product."

"Each product is slightly different and has its own unique characteristics making them *one-of-a-kind* pieces."

"This is what I call "*heirloom quality*"—reinforced, double-stitched and very soundly made. If you take care of it, you can pass it on to your children . . . and even your grandchildren!"

"I use only the *very best materials*."

"This is a *collectible* series. Many of my customers collect this series and showcase them in glass cases."

This may seem a bit much, but if you spread the phrases out a little and don't use every one of them too often—just the ones that apply to your particular products—they work very well.

How to Close a Sale

The customer has the product in her hand, but she still seems a bit undecided. She is weighing the pros and cons. She is not walking toward you or your sales area yet; she is still thinking about it. This is an important moment for you. The sale could go either way at this point. There's a very real chance your customer could put the product down and walk away. What can you do to encourage the sale?

Though I have said over and over again that you shouldn't press the customer, here I will make an exception. It is time to give your customer a nudge. If you don't *ask* for the sale, you may not get it. A phrase such as "Would you like me to wrap that for you?" will encourage a reaction in your favor. It may be all you need to close this sale. *Ask* your customer for that final commitment. If the customer is not quite ready to make up her mind, she will most likely tell you what her reservations are about buying your product. Then you can step in and help her make up her mind.

If the customer is having difficulty deciding between two products, you might say, "Which one would you like?" At best, this will put her on the spot to make a decision. If it doesn't, at least she will tell you why she can't make up her mind. Then you will have a chance to offer a solution.

You don't have the luxury of spending all of your time with just one customer while they vacillate between buying and not buying. Eventually if they don't make a move, you will have to take the initiative. Ask for the sale. More often than not, you'll get it.

What to Say After the Sale

Customers who buy from you once are likely to purchase from you again. They like your *products*. They like your *craft*. They like your *style*. They like your *prices*. Whatever feature made them buy that first product could lead to future sales. While you are packaging a customer's purchase, set the groundwork for future sales. Ask your customers to sign your mailing list. Make sure you have a record of each and every person who buys a product from you or who expresses a serious interest in your products. Then you can send them information on upcoming shows and new products you might develop that they would like.

Encourage customers to look for you again at other crafts shows. Have copies of your future show schedule on hand and distribute them to your customers. Include them when you package your customers' purchases. If you know where your customer lives, you might say, "I'll be showing in your town on May 23 at the Armory. It's a nice show—you should come."

Give them something to look forward to when they see you again—"I'm planning a special series of these in the spring," "This is the last year I will be selling this doll—there'll be a new edition in the fall," "Though right now I only work with *silver*, next month I will introduce a line of reasonably priced gold jewelry." Tell your customers about the future direction of your business. They just might be interested.

Customers buying my product will usually keep the product for many years. Unless it is somehow damaged beyond repair, or the customer re-decorates her home, the product will not need not be replaced. How can I hope for future business from these customers? I suggest that my product is a wonderful and thoughtful *gift* item for their mother, a newly married friend or relative who probably won't have one (What a great shower or wedding gift!), their married children, friends and neighbors, or as a housewarming gift for a new home-buyer. These are applications they probably never though of. Ah, the power of suggestion . . .

If your product is such that people usually only buy one of them, then it is up to you to suggest other applications. Give your customers a reason to buy from you in the future. I had one customer who, after purchasing one of my products, came back the following year and bought one for each of her married daughters—five in all.

Future sales are as important to you as current sales. You are setting the stage and laying the foundation necessary to *expand* your crafts business, to keep old customers coming back while still developing new ones. Take every opportunity to do so.

Don't be discouraged if your initial attempts at conversation do not result in a sale. It takes a little practice to know the right thing to say—and to say it right. The more you speak to your customers, the faster you will learn what to say to encourage the sale. What should be the very last thing you say to your customer? Thank you! For indeed, where would you be without them?

One Final Word

Your customers are your most valuable asset. Respect them. Though I have shown you many ways to make your products and yourself *look* more valuable to your customers, please make sure they truly are. The messages you communicate, the perceptions you cultivate not only reflect on you and your products, but on the entire crafts industry at large. Market your products with sincerity and honesty—and with pride.

More Great Books for Crafters!

How to Make Enchanting Miniature Teddy Bears—Create adorable little bears with fuzzy fabric, a snippet of thread and the step-by-step instructions you'll find in this handy reference. Ten illustrated projects take you through a range of projects—from a simple teddy bear pin to a range of teddies with different styles and moveable limbs. #30846/$22.99/128 pages/212 color illus./paperback

The Paper Card Book—Now you can make more than fifty card designs using gift wrap, ticket stubs, maps and more! These easy and fun-to-make designs can hold photos and mementos, fold-out, pop-up—even close with a button. Plus, step-by-step techniques will help you create your own personalized designs with tips on choosing papers, measuring, designing and adding finishing touches. #30982/$19.99/96 pages/200 color illus./paperback

Make Your Quilting Pay for Itself—Go from hobbyist to professional with guidance from fiber arts specialist and businesswoman, Sylvia Landman! You'll learn the essence of careful planning—from finding a niche to setting appropriate fees to crafty marketing. Plus, nine professional quilters share their success stories so you can follow in their footsteps! #70373/$18.99/144 pages/11 b&w illus./paperback

Easy Airbrush Projects for Crafters & Decorative Painters—Using the airbrush for crafts and decorative painting has never been easier! You'll get the inside story on getting started in airbrushing and basic painting techniques. Then, move on to 10 step-by-step projects that perfect what you've learned. #30908/$23.99/128 pages/356 color, 18 b&w illus./paperback

The Crafter's Guide to Pricing Your Work—Price and sell more than 75 kinds of crafts with this must-have reference. You'll learn how to set prices to maximize income while maintaining a fair profit margin. Includes tips on record-keeping, consignment, taxes, reducing costs and managing your cash flow. #70353/$16.99/160 pages/paperback

Creating Extraordinary Beads From Ordinary Materials—Transform run-of-the-mill materials into uncommonly beautiful beads! No experience or fancy equipment is required—just follow 53 step-by-step projects to get great results using everyday materials like construction paper, fabric scraps, yarn and more! #30905/$22.99/128 pages/326 color, 18 b&w illus./paperback

Crafts Marketplace: Where and How to Sell Your Crafts—Make a profit with your fine products! You'll discover more than 560 shows, craft malls, cooperatives and other places to market your work. Then, you'll be guided through every step of successfully selling your wares—from start-up through sales! #70335/$18.99/336 pages/paperback

Selling Your Dolls and Teddy Bears: A Complete Guide—Earn as you learn the business, public relations and legal aspects of doll and teddy bear sales. Some of the most successful artists in the business share the nitty-gritty details of pricing, photographing, tax planning, customer relations and more! #70352/$18.99/160 pages/31 b&w illus./paperback

How to Start Making Money With Your Crafts—Launch a rewarding crafts business with this guide that starts with the basics—

from creating marketable products to setting the right prices—and explores all the exciting possibilities. End-of-chapter quizzes, worksheets, ideas and lessons learned by successful crafters are included to increase your learning curve. #70302/$18.99/176 pages/35 b&w illus./paperback

Painting & Decorating Birdhouses—Turn unfinished birdhouses into something special—from a quaint Victorian roost to a Southwest pueblo, from a rustic log cabin to a lighthouse! These colorful and easy decorative painting projects are for the birds with 22 clever projects to create indoor decorative birdhouses, as well as functional ones to grace your garden. #30882/$23.99/128 pages/194 color illus./paperback

Painting Houses, Cottages and Towns on Rocks—Turn ordinary rocks into charming cottages, country churches and Victorian mansions! Accomplished artist Lin Wellford shares 11 fun, inexpensive, step-by-step projects that are sure to please. #30823/$21.99/128 pages/398 color illus./paperback

Making Greeting Cards With Rubber Stamps—Discover hundreds of quick, creative, stamp-happy ways to make extra-special cards—no experience, fancy equipment or expensive materials required! You'll find 30 easy-to-follow projects for holidays, birthdays, thank you's and more! #30821/$21.99/128 pages/231 color illus./paperback

How to Make Clay Characters—Bring cheery clay characters to life! The creator of collectible clay "Pippsywoggins" figures shares her fun and easy techniques for making adorable little figures—no sculpting experience required! #30881/$22.99/128 pages/579 color illus./paperback

Making Books by Hand—Discover 12 beautiful projects for making handmade albums, scrapbooks, journals and more. Only everyday items like cardboard, wrapping paper and ribbon are needed to make these exquisite books for family and friends. #30942/$24.99/108 pages/250 color illus.

Make It With Paper Series—Discover loads of bright ideas and easy-to-do projects for making colorful paper creations. Includes paper to cut and fold, templates and step-by-step instructions for designing your own creations. Plus, each paperback book has over 200-300 color illustrations to lead you along the way.
    Paper Flowers—#30965/$19.99/72 pages
    Paper Animals—#30966/$19.99/72 pages
    Paper Boxes—#30935/$19.99/114 pages
    Paper Pop-Ups—#30936/$19.99/96 pages

The Decorative Stamping Sourcebook—Embellish walls, furniture, fabric and accessories—with stamped designs! You'll find 180 original, traceable motifs in a range of themes and illustrated instructions for making your own stamps to enhance any decorating style. #30898/$24.99/128 pages/200 color illus.

Make Jewelry Series—With basic materials and a little creativity you can make great-looking jewelry! Each 96-page paperback book contains 15 imaginative projects using materials from clay to fabric to paper—and over 200 color illustrations to make jewelry creation a snap!
    Barrettes & More—#30963/$15.99
    Make Pins—#30964/$15.99
    Make Bracelets—#30939/$15.99
    Make Earrings—#30940/$15.99
    Make Necklaces—#30941/$15.99

The Doll Sourcebook—Bring your dolls and supplies as close as the telephone with this unique sourcebook of retailers, artists, restorers, appraisers and more! Each listing contains extensive information—from addresses and phone numbers to business hours and product lines. #70325/$22.99/352 pages/176 b&w illus./paperback

The Art of Painting Animals on Rocks—Discover how a dash of paint can turn humble stones into charming "pet rocks." This hands-on, easy-to-follow book offers a menagerie of fun—and potentially profitable—stone animal projects. Eleven examples, complete with materials lists, photos of the finished piece and patterns will help you create a forest of fawns, rabbits, foxes and other adorable critters. #30606/$21.99/144 pages/250 color illus./paperback

The Crafts Supply Sourcebook: A Comprehensive Shop-by-Mail Guide, 4th Edition—Turn here to find the materials you need—from specialty tools and the hardest-to-find accessories, to clays, doll parts, patterns, quilting machines and hundreds of other items! Listings organized by area of interest make it quick and easy! #70344/$18.99/320 pages/paperback

The Teddy Bear Sourcebook: For Collectors and Artists—Discover the most complete treasury of bear information stuffed between covers. You'll turn here whenever you need to find sellers of bear making supplies, major manufacturers of teddy bears, teddy bear shows, auctions and contests, museums that house teddy bear collections and much more. #70294/$18.99/356 pages/202 illus./paperback

DISCARD